You Can Quote Me on That

You Can Quote Me on That

Wit, Wisdom, Wickedness and Waffle of Modern Ireland

Compiled by Aubrey Malone

CURRACH
PRESS

First published in 2008 by
CURRACH PRESS
55A Spruce Avenue, Stillorgan Industrial Park, Blackrock, Co. Dublin
www.currach.ie

1 3 5 4 2

Cover by Bluett
Origination by Currach Press
Printed by ColourBooks, Baldoyle Industrial Estate, Dublin 13
ISBN: 978-1-85607-964-8
The author has asserted his moral rights.

Contents

POLITICAL ANIMALS

I can't see myself ever running for president. I wouldn't want to move to a smaller house.

Joe Duffy

Did you ever notice how you never see Bertie Ahern and Mary Harney together? That's because there *is* no Mary Harney. It's Bertie dressed up. Everyone in the Dáil's known about it for years but it's all hushed up. One day he's the Taoiseach, the next he puts on the wig and the dress and he's the Tánaiste. It's a big scam to claim two Dáil salaries.

Paul Howard

There are lies, damned lies, and Fianna Fáil party political broadcasts.

Barry Desmond

Oppositions don't win elections. Governments lose them.

Eamon Dunphy

David Trimble wants to 'park' the Good Friday Agreement. Normally when you park something it gets vandalised.

Bertie Ahern in 1999

We in Northern Ireland are not Irish. We do not speak Gaelic, play GAA or jig at crossroads.

John Taylor

They say my donkey laugh can be heard in the next county.

John Bruton

Éamon de Valera was the bastard son of a Spanish ukulele player from the Bronx.

Eamonn Keane

My mother used to say, 'Everyone hates Charlie Haughey except the people.'

Seán Haughey

A TD was asked to join the Cabinet so he phoned his wife. 'How would you like to be the wife of a Cabinet minister?' he asked. 'Which one?' she answered.

Myler McGrath

Earlier this year, George Bush was looking to put Saddam Hussein in a place Where he would never threaten anyone. So he put him in the Mayo forward line.

Pat Spillane in 2004

The difficult part is *becoming* Taoiseach. The easy part is *being* Taoiseach.

Enda Kenny

Bertie Ahern is a humble man with a lot to be humble about.

Eoghan Harris

The reason I got out of politics was because I had four children and none of them knew who I was.

Ivan Yates

The politics business involves long hours and intense work, including the running of clinics hand-shaking, funeral-going and the purchase of raffle-tickets.

Gene Kerrigan

The Irish population is mainly made up of young people, many of whom find politics as boring as algebra, or Julie Andrews.

Terry Eagleton

I was warned by Sinn Féin that I shouldn't mention punishment beatings. I'm a priest, for fuck's sake. What do they expect?

Sinéad O'Connor

We're horrified. Did Pádraig Pearse, Peter O'Toole and Eugene Lambert have to die in the GPO on Pancake Tuesday 1916 only to have the Brits singing their anthem in Croker's hallowed ground some ninety years later?

Podge and Rodge on the controversial rugby match between Ireland and England in Croke Park in February 2007

Safe seats are occupied by bottoms that sit on fences.

Liz O'Donnell

I rarely hear a discussion on politics without somebody saying, 'The jury is still out on that one.' I wish they would stay out and never come back.

Con Houlihan

There are few topics more prone to hypocrisy than environmentalism. I hear savage attacks on George Bush's failure to sign the Kyoto Treaty by people who have three cars sitting in their drive: his, hers, and the stay-home twenty-somethings.

Mary Kenny

Fianna Fáil aren't only unsure who to go to bed with any more, they can hardly remember where they live. Perhaps they think that if they keep wandering around those Ring Roads they'll eventually find the old homestead, and hope to Christ that the key still fits.

Declan Lynch

I once told Richard Bruton he was too nice for politics. 'I know,' he replied, 'I carry it around with me like a wooden leg.'

Olivia O'Leary

The presidency is a bit-like being in a goldfish bowl on top of a pedestal.

Mary Robinson

Women don't vote for women. Most of them vote for me.

Bertie Ahern

What Michael McDowell would call a New Deal, I would call a raw deal.

Michael D. Higgins

Government propaganda is like the Met Office claiming credit for fine weather.

Ivan Yates

Bless me, listeners, for I have sinned. I once asked a politician to do me a favour.

Olivia O'Leary

Pádraig Pearse's direct descendants wear scarves, beads, wristbands, and drive Mitsubishis. I also now know where the tall, skinny man who used to sell *In Dublin* outside Bewley's for many years is these days. He is dropping his daughter to school. It is more Celtic Twilight than economic dawn.

David McWilliams

Only in Ireland could a woman as overweight as Mary Harney be Minister for Health.

Des Bishop

The trouble with a gentleman's agreement is that it has to be between gentlemen.

Michael McDowell

Patriotic Paddy is often seen wearing a moss-green Aran sweater. He bought it in British Home Stores but cut the label off and tells people it was knitted in Armagh Women's Prison.

Anne Marie Scanlon

Al Gore is so boring he makes dishwater look thrilling.

Helen O'Hara

I wouldn't tolerate anyone forming kebabs within Fianna Fáil.

Bertie Ahern

Robert Kilroy-Silk once called Ray McSharry a 'redundant, second-rate politician from a country peopled by priests, peasants and pixies'. Everybody agreed that it was an incredibly stupid thing to say as there are no pixies in Ireland, only leprechauns.

David Kenny

William Binchy is a very clever man, but then so was Hitler.

Ruairí Quinn

I once heard a student debater claim that the root cause of all the problems in the Middle East was that 'Israel was a stupid place to put a country.'

Abie Philbin Bowman

Once you become a TD and you've figured out which asses to kiss, you're ambitious, presentable and articulate, you appear to have more than half a brain and you're sober at least three days out of seven, the chances of being appointed to office are very good indeed.

Gene Kerrigan

The O'Malleys are a small, black-haired species of politician who thrive in the damp marshlands around the river Shannon and speak through their noses. Once every five years they emerge from the safety of their habitat to poke fun at Willie O'Dea and speak down to the people of Limerick – through their noses.

Pat Fitzpatrick

The Catholic Church introduced me to Marxism. It's the happiest memory I have of school.

Joe O'Connor

Michael McDowell wrestled with his conscience, and his conscience won.

Pat Rabbitte

The land of 100,000 Welcomes is fast becoming the land of 100,000 Thieves.

Sean Barrett

I'm one of the few socialists left in Irish politics.

Bertie Ahern

The reason there are so few female politicians is that it takes too much time to put make-up on two faces.

Maureen Murphy

What side your great grandfather took in the Civil War still determines many people's political allegiances in the 21st century.

Liam Collins

Politicians are like nappies. They should be changed often – and for the same reason.

Pat Shortt

Politicians sometimes suggest Ireland is richer than Germany. If this is the case, why do they not also have crowded A&E wards and creaking 1930s hospitals crawling with MRSA?

David McWilliams

It was my actions that caused the setting up of the tribunals. That makes me feel like a complete bloody eejit.

Ben Dunne

They were going to get me to turn the lights on in Belfast last Christmas but they changed their minds at the last minute because when the last person called Paddy was asked to press a button in Belfast, the whole of Bedford Street went up.

Patrick Kielty

You just hit the nail on the hammer.

Dick Roche

I'll be an old man before the tribunal is finished with me.

Bertie Ahern

I believe Sinn Féin are amalgamating with the Green Party. They're going to call themselves Guns & Roses.

Conal Gallen

I read in the paper that Bertie Ahern is going to 'buck' up the economy. There has to be a misprint there somewhere.

Maureen Potter

Unless he's reading from a script, George Bush is entirely unable to make sense of the English language.

Donal Lynch

After Garret Fitzgerald finished explaining to me about 800 years of British oppression, I felt I had been through the entire time myself.

Margaret Thatcher

I have a recurring dream of sleeping with Tina Turner.

Jackie Healy-Rae

The Minister for Finance has simplified tax forms. They now have only two questions: 1: 'How much do you earn?' and 2: 'Send it forthwith.'

Myler McGrath

I've always thought that in the scenario of Bertie Ahern and Mary Harney getting into bed together, Michael McDowell would be the brooding presence on the bedpost.

Pat Rabbitte

My specialty is omniscience.

Charles Haughey

I work fast. I've had people with me in my clinics on a Friday morning who said they had a letter from me before they got home.

Ivor Callelly

Japanese scientists have created a camera with such a fast shutter speed that they can now photograph Garret Fitzgerald with his mouth shut.

John Scally

The reason I probably can't give you a better reflection of what I was doing on 19 January is because I didn't do it.

Bertie Ahern at the Mahon Tribunal in September 2007

As you might have guessed from their double-barrelled surname, the Healy-Raes are actually a wealthy Anglo-Irish family who only act like cartoon bogmen because they watched *Killinascully* to ascertain how the Irish actually behave.

Pat Fitzpatrick

I realised I was finally become fully Irish when, the more I realised Fianna Fáil were corrupt, the more I wanted to vote for them.

Des Bishop

The PDs need to be more like Dunnes and less like Superquinn.

Michael Cullen

Is our Bertie corruptible? He of the penitent Lenten smudge on his forehead, with his humble man's pint of Bass and shy Princess Di smile, tending his hanging baskets at All Hallows, the house he still calls home?

Justine McCarthy

Chelsea Clinton has more teeth than a Ferrari gearbox.

Patrick Kielty

I find it hard to believe that Bertie Ahern can't recollect driving Celia Larkin down to the AIB in O'Connell Street in 1995 to withdraw €50,000. Surely anyone who found a parking space in O'Connell Street, even in the mid-1990s would remember it.

Brendan Casserly

Communism bothers me. They have nothing and they want to share it with us.

Hal Roach

I blame the Anglo-Irish Agreement for Sunday drinking.

Ian Paisley

The higher up the tree you go, the more you show your arse.

Maurice Dockrell

Charlie Haughey could switch from charm to nastiness in the blink of his hooded eyes. 'If you come close with that again I'll shove it down your fuckin' throat!' was a typical offering when my microphone drifted too close to his face.

Fergal Keane

There are certain times when it seems that this country is grimly intent on backsliding into the bad old days when the Irish simply refused to believe the evidence in front of their eyes. One example is the way Bertie Ahern can be exposed as either corrupt or a beggar in the wake of his marriage breakup…and see his ratings rise.

Ian O'Doherty

Thirty years in Dáil Éireann and never opened his mouth except to pick his teeth.

John B. Keane

I'm all for giving politicians a pay rise. Cocaine costs a fortune these days.

Sean Hughes

Politics is so corrupt, even dishonest people get fucked.

George Carlin

When I was in the White House one day I ran into Martin McGuinness and he said to me, 'Bryan Dobson from RTE! Janey, they'd let anyone in here these days'.

Bryan Dobson

Everyone's entitled to my opinion.

Charles Haughey

David 'Just Call Me Dave' Cameron has somehow managed the incredible knack of being nothing to all men.

Ian O'Doherty

When you get to the top in politics, you stop plotting. And the minute you stop plotting you start going down.

Katie Hannon

George Bush is all for allowing illegal immigrants to stay in America. I know why. Everyone else hates him.

Des Bishop

Mary Harney isn't the Minister for Health. She's the Minister for Trolleys.

Noel Healy

I'm looking for the shadow Minister for Health in the 'Lost and Found' column.

Brendan Gleeson

I'd love to do a memoir, but a lot of people will have to be dead first.

Máire Geoghegan-Quinn

The Male–Female Thing

Women. Can't live with them; can't live with them.

Dylan Moran

I was once engaged to a man who was very good to his mother. That impressed me. I was always told that a man will treat his wife like he treats his mother. We broke up when he told me he wanted to bring her on the honeymoon.

Teresa Gaffney

Some are born girls and some have girliness thrust upon them.

Róisín Ingle

I've dated lots of Italian girls and I'd hate to generalise about them. But they're all mad.

Ian O'Doherty

I once tried to French-kiss a girl in the Gaeltacht and my tongue got caught in her dental brace.

Joe O'Connor

I've lost 40 pounds since Christmas – 150 if you include the wife.

David Feherty after his divorce

If golf WAGS behaved like soccer ones, the Ryder Cup would have to be re-named the Ride Her Cup.

Liam O'Mahony

My first date wasn't approved of. I left Senior Infants under a cloud.

Frank Kelly

I tried phone sex once but it didn't work. I got my penis stuck in the nine.

Kevin Meaney

Sometimes it's hard to be a woman. There's so much to remember: Whiten your teeth, visit a nail bar, iron your hair, fake bake your legs, have Botox injections and eyelash injections, lie to your friends about the Botox.

Martina Devlin

I once had an almighty row with a boyfriend because I wanted to watch a documentary on the Playboy mansion and he wanted to watch *Ally McBeal*. When he threatened to burn my Cork football jersey I gave in.

Siobhán Cronin

The great thing about being single is that you can do what you want when you want. The bad thing is that you've got nothing to do and no one to do it with.

James O'Loughlin

I'm only a woman on Tuesdays.

Anne Enright

What would you call a man chatting up Sonia O'Sullivan? Someone trying to pull a fast one.

Donal McLaughlin

It's got easy being a man. I had to get dressed today. And there are also other pressures.

Dylan Moran

Murphy threw up on the plane and the air hostess was outraged. 'There's a bag in front of you,' she said, 'Why didn't you use that?' 'I don't even know the woman,' Murphy replied.

Conal Gallen

Attending an all-girls school had its advantages. For one thing, you didn't have to worry about how you looked in the mornings.

Dana

Young people are good to look at and fun to fuck, but there's nothing going on upstairs.

Dara O'Briain

American women have this ambivalent attitude towards their men. They want to screw them and at the same time they want to castrate them.

George Best

Anyone who believes the way to a man's heart is through his stomach flunked geography.

Robert O'Byrne

Men use toilets to pee. For women they're social clubs.

Brendan O'Carroll

They say never go to bed mad. With this in mind, my wife and I once stayed up for six months.

Brendan Grace

Women see things that men don't: dirt, relatives, bargains.

Dylan Moran

Why does the word 'spinster' sound so much worse than 'bachelor'?

Ryan Tubridy

Whenever I read the papers about my love life I go 'Who's she? She's obviously having a ball.'

Andrea Corr

I was the sixth of seven children. My mother cordially disliked my father. I wonder how many they might have had if she'd liked him!

Vincent Dowling

If they ever invent a vibrator that mows that lawn, that'll be the end of us men.

Dave Allen

Older men and younger women – it's been around since the Old Testament. Eve would never have stood a chance with Adam if there hadn't only been the two of them in the Garden of Eden.

Martina Devlin

My mother believes there should be more women in male-dominated jobs. I thought she would be pleased I got a post as a petrol pump attendant, but I think she would have preferred brain surgery.

Katy Hayes

Once people reach the age of forty, they should be barred from using the words 'girlfriend' and 'boyfriend' in reference to someone they're fucking.

George Carlin

I saw this ad in a lad mag: 'Man looking For Woman For Fun Time. Age 20 to 60.' Know who I felt sorry for? The 61 year old women reading it.

Sean Hughes

All gay men have this weird relationship with their mums, because they want to be her a little bit.

Brendan Courtney

Men will come and men will go, but there will always be shoes.

Marian Keyes

I had a long-term relationship with a young Muslim girl and, you know, even today I often wonder what she looked like.

Ian McPherson

My wife asked me to buy her something with diamonds. I got her a deck of cards.

Brendan O'Carroll

It was widely said among my counterparts that Protestant girls were the best because they let you go all the way.

Fergal Keane

After four decades of onslaught from feminism, the western male is a beaten docket.

John Waters

Irish women like the simple things in life – like Irish men

Mary Coughlan

I have this wonderful mistress called The Gate.

Michael Colgan

A line that should never be used for ending a relationship is, 'I don't think I'm ready for a relationship yet.' So what were you doing in this one?

Robert O'Byrne

Who needs a man when you have undiagnosed chlamydia, nascent late-onset alcoholism, and a forty-year mortgage?

Martha Connolly

If women ran the world there'd be less wars. They'd be too busy re-arranging countries. It'd be, like, 'Where do you think the Statue of Liberty should go?'

Michael Downey

Why do Dublin footballers ride ladies' bicycles? Because they have difficulty getting their balls over the bar.

Pat Spillane

I asked this girl how she liked her eggs in the morning. 'Unfertilised,' she replied.

Milo O'Shea

I met Monica Bellucci in Lillie's. Marched straight up to her and I was like, 'I've lost my phone number – can I borrow yours?' Corny, I know, but she fell for it. There wasn't much going on upstairs. As Fionn said, she thinks Sugar Diabetes is a Welsh middleweight boxer.

Ross O'Carroll Kelly

Cupid isn't picky about where he shoots his arrows. I know one girl whose parents met over a septic tank.

Anne Marie Scanlon

Irish women rule. Who's the only politician with the guts to stand up to the Church? Liz O'Donnell. Who were the only people in recent years with the guts to stand up to the IRA in their heartland? The McCartney sisters. Who's the best stage actress in Britain? Fiona Shaw. Who told us what to eat? Darina Allen. What's the one book which haunts us from our schooldays? *Peig*. What's the most memorable passage in our national novel? Molly Bloom's monologue.

Eamonn Sweeney

If we're really to believe women when they say the most important quality in a man is a sense of humour, why doesn't Angelina Jolie dump Brad Pitt for Woody Allen?

Graham Norton

Sex is important but fun is essential.

Terry Prone

A girl should hang on to her youth, but not while he's driving.

Seamus O'Leary

Stacking the dishwasher represents my commitment to my marriage.

George Hook

Oh, the platonic bridges we've burnt in the name of not going home alone.

Róisín Ingle

Friendship is more generous than love in many ways. I like my friends to have other friends, but I wouldn't like my lover to have other lovers.

Maeve Binchy

Here's the history of male-female relationships in a sentence: Women always worry about the things men forget, and men always worry about the things women remember.

Niall Toibin

These days it's easier to pull in Woodies than Lillies.

David McWilliams

I don't have any role models, just loads of models.

Eddie Irvine

A woman has the last word in any argument. Anything a man says after that is the beginning of a new argument.

Paul O'Farrell

When Colin Farrell was seeing Britney Spears, he was doing it for all of us.

Dara O'Briain

James Joyce liked to believe a woman was an animal who micturates once a day, defecates once a week, menstruates once a month, and parturates once a year.

Edna O'Brien

I'm a modern man so I have no problem buying tampons. Unfortunately women don't consider them a proper present.

Jimmy Carr

Not at all. If she dies, she dies!

Michael Colgan after being asked if he was worried about the age gap between himself and his – substantially younger – girlfriend Noelle

I don't have a girlfriend at the moment, I'm engaged to Inter Milan.

Robbie Keane in 2000

There's an ideal woman for every man in this world – and he's bloody lucky if his wife doesn't find out about her.

Conal Gallen

My best mate's girlfriend is six months pregnant, She said to me, 'Do you want to feel the baby?' On reflection I think she meant on the outside.

Jimmy Carr

Pascal was our French student lodger. He used to follow my mother around the kitchen practising his phrases. 'You are very beautiful woman. I would much like to passionately make love with you.' Pascal was twelve. This infuriated my father. He said, 'For God's sake, Pascal, how many times do I have to tell you? Don't. Split. Infinitives.'

Ian McPherson

The best cure for a hangover is to find a good book and go to bed with it. Better still, find a woman who reads a good book to you.

David Feherty

I told my mother I was disgusted with my boyfriend because he was two-timing me. 'Which one?' she asked.

Andrea O'Connor

Men love women with curves. Do you really think they'd choose stick-insect Victoria over the hour-glass-shaped Nigella Lawson?

Siobhán Hegarty

The one thing men could do with a little helpful advice on is apologising. They don't like doing it and they're rotten at it when there's no alternative.

Terry Prone

Regrettable Utterances

He died in his sleep so he doesn't know he's dead yet. If he wakes up, the shock will kill him.

Biddie McGrath

I always get letters from people when I call Galway a town instead of a city, although I never do.

John Bowman

The Spanish manager is pulling his captain off.

George Hamilton

Culture Club never actually split up. We just stopped speaking to each other and went our separate ways.

Boy George

The best way to pass a cow on the road when cycling is to keep behind it.

R.J. Macready

Never has my flabber been so totally gasted.

David Feherty after watching a brilliant shot played by Tiger Woods

I didn't have an unhappy childhood, but I was an unhappy child.

John Connolly

He hasn't made any saves you wouldn't have expected him not to make.

Liam Brady

This is Vicente Fernandez of Argentina. You'll notice that he walks with a slight limp. This is because he was born with one leg shorter than the other two.

Roddy Carr

According to my son, trigonometry is having three wives at a time.

Shona Tubridy

Then there was the fella who got a job in the Ohio State Penitentiary and was asked to have a look at the electric chair, which was malfunctioning. After pulling it apart he said to the governor, 'You're lucky you called me out. That thing is a death trap.'

Noel V. Ginnity

And now as we come to the news at 1.30, I'm afraid we have to leave Harry Belafonte with his hole in the bucket.

Treasa Davidson

The problems at Wimbledon seem to be that the club has suffered a loss of complacency.

Joe Kinnear

I knew this man and his doctor gave him two weeks to live. The man said, 'Could I have the last week in June and the first week in July?'

Paul Malone

I was going to kill myself by taking a bottle of aspirin but after the first two I felt much better.

Seamus O'Leary

I once went into a bookshop and asked if they stocked *Confessions of Saint Augustine*. The assistant said to me, 'Who is it by?'

Hugh Leonard

Welcome to the Nou Camp Stadium in Barcelona, which is packed to capacity with some patches of seats left empty.

George Hamilton

A woman once told me on my radio show that she'd love to give Omar Sharif mouth-to-mouth recitation.

Gay Byrne

I don't think it helps people to start throwing white elephants and red herrings at each other.

Bertie Ahern

Over the years a lot of great players have left United. I'm sure the same will happen to me one day.

Roy Keane

It was the sort of goal that made your hair stand on your shoulders.

Niall Quinn

It's *déjà vu* all over again.

George Hamilton

The biggest influence in my life was the Tech in Ballyfermot, which is the school I didn't go to.

Joe Duffy

Gone To Lunch. Back in Five Minutes. Signed: Godot.

Sign spotted in a Mayo café

I remember going into Terry Brady's shop in Fairyhouse some years ago to buy some of his delicious buns. I came out with a motorised buggy. On another occasion I went in for an ice cream and came out with a chainsaw.

Sean Boylan

Whenever I order a pizza over the phone and give Áras an Uachtaráin as my address, they hang up.

Mary McAleese

If the fourth official had done his job it wouldn't have happened, but I don't want to blame anyone.

John Aldridge

Most players would give their right arm for his left foot.

Mark Lawrenson on Jason Wilcox

I have no recollection of my grandfather, who died before I was born.

Gloria Hunniford

The doctor gave my father six months to live. When he couldn't pay the bill he gave him another six.

Dusty Young

Yesterday I thought I saw my brother on the street and he also thought he saw me, but when both of us got up close we realised it was neither of us.

Shane McCarthy

What do you call women who practise the rhythm method of birth control? Parents.

Peter O'Toole

He's got a knock on his shin there, just above the knee.

Frank Stapleton

What it lacks in excitement it makes up for in its complete lack of excitement.

Dara O'Briain

This play will be repeated tomorrow night, so that those who missed it before will have an opportunity of doing so again.

Sign outside a theatre in Dublin

If crime went down 100%, it would still be fifty times higher than it should be.

John Bowman

Does your epileptic fit…or would you have to take it in a bit at the sides?

Jason Byrne

Any team is only as strong as its weakest link, and that's been our strength throughout – there hasn't been a weak link.

Mark Lawrenson

I would never condemn wrongdoing.

Bertie Ahern

These managers all know their onions and cut their cloth accordingly.

Mark Lawrenson

I wouldn't mind the rain if it wasn't for the wet.

Jimmy O'Dea

The crowd gave the players an arousing reception.

Packie Bonner

Hindsight is always 50–50.

Bertie Ahern

I thought I was wrong but I was mistaken.

Dan O'Herlihy

I bet I can make you give up gambling.

Anthony Bluett

Which side went out to retaliate first?

Danny Blanchflower

Send your answers on a postcard. The winner will be the first one opened.

Liam Campbell

If Ireland finish with a draw in winning the game, that would be fine.

Jack Charlton

If golf wasn't my living I wouldn't play it if you paid me.

Christy O'Connor

When I'm in a wig I'm pretty attractive. I stare at myself in mirrors because I'm my type.

Kevin McDonald

They say you only use 10% of your brain. What about the other 10%?

Sil Fox

The foot is on the other feets.

Bertie Ahern

Mickey Joe made his championship début in such a way that he will never be asked to make it again.

John B. Keane

Ireland will give 99% – everything they've got.

Mark Lawrenson

A woman asked me for my autograph once. 'What name will I put on it?' I said to her. 'Your own!' she replied.

Gabriel Byrne

We Irish take our golf seriously, but we have fun taking it seriously.

Mary McAleese

I hate not being invited to parties I wouldn't be seen dead at.

Christina Moriarity

I don't believe in giving up smoking. I've never been a quitter.

Peter O'Toole

Paul Scholes has four players in front of him – five if you count Gary Neville.

Darragh Maloney

We're now going to Wembley for live second half commentary on the England–Scotland game except that it's at Hampden Park.

Eamon Andrews

If I don't get the contract I want I won't sign it, but that's not a threat.

Roy Keane

We shouldn't upset the apple tart.

Bertie Ahern

I'll throttle the next person who accuses me of being violent.

Kevin McAleer

It's a no-win game for us, although I suppose we can win by winning.

Gary Doherty

He's not the sharpest sandwich in the picnic.

Tony Cascarino

Beware: To Touch These Wires Is Instant Death. Anyone Found Doing So Will Be Prosecuted.

Sign at a Donegal Electric Station

I was both surprised and delighted to take the armband for both legs.

Gary O'Neill

The groin's a little sore but after the semi-final I put it to the back of my head.

Michael Hughes

I was staring into the middle distance in the café, trying to work something out in my mind. 'Cheer up, it might never happen,' a man said to me. I told him it wasn't like that at all. I'm simply trying to work out what colour my rasher is.'

Pat Ingoldsby

The first half was even. The second half was even worse.

Pat Spillane

A medical friend once took Samuel Beckett for a walk in the Dublin hills, hoping to cheer him up. 'It's a beautiful day,' said the friend. 'Oh it's all right,' grunted the writer. 'No,' insisted the medic, 'it's the sort of day that makes you feel glad to be alive.' To which Beckett snapped, 'I wouldn't go that far.'

Declan Kiberd

The Koreans were quicker in terms of speed.

Mark Lawrenson

We will be an aggressive opposition where we oppose things, and we'll support things that we support,

Bertie Ahern

I like going to doctors so they can investigate me for diseases I don't have.

Tommy Tiernan

Personally I have no bone to pick with graveyards.

Samuel Beckett

He had been sentenced to death but saved his life by dying in jail.

Tony Butler

I enjoyed going to the toilet in Buckingham Palace. It's nice to feel you've been able to leave something behind.

Gloria Hunniford

Achilles tendons are a pain in the butt.

David O'Leary

There was a bit of retaliation there, though not actually on the same player.

Frank Stapleton

When I was young my whole family used to sit around the television for hours. Eventually my grandfather would say, 'Will we turn it on?'

Kevin McAleer

The God-Shaped Hole

A Jehovah Witness knocked on the door of a man's house in the country and was invited in for tea and sandwiches. As he was pouring the tea the man said, 'Now tell me all about Jehovah.' The Jehovah's Witness replied, 'I know nothing about him. I've never got this far before.'

Noel V. Ginnity

My housekeeper is a Baptist. My doctor is a Jew. My lawyer is a Congregationalist. My secretary is a Presbyterian. My wife is a convert. I have four Catholic kids and six Catholic grandchildren. I'm looking for some atheist friends.

Pat O'Brien

I believe in God in times of pain and mortal danger.

Martin Malone

I'm what you'd call ethnically Catholic. Don't believe in God, still hate Rangers.

Dara O'Briain

Ireland has been turned upside down. Protestants are calling their kids Fiach and living in semi-ds and Catholics are baking scones and insisting on period furniture only.

David McWilliams

We went to confession to Fr Ryan, who had a hearing problem. We whispered our sins in spite of his repeated requests to 'Speak up, my son'. We were happy in the knowledge that he gave everybody three Hail Marys for penance. Needless to say, all the sinners were to be found outside his Confessional.

Donal McKenna

The Catholic Church is a crazy organisation under an evil regime.

Dave Fanning

There's one big difference between a priest and a stand-up comic. Stand-up comics have to make up different jokes for each gig.

Des Bishop

The Catholic religion is a beautiful fairy story for children.

Patrick Kavanagh

Saint Patrick was a Protestant.

Ian Paisley

Easter is cancelled – they found the body.

Graffiti

I'm a Catholic atheist rather than a Protestant one.

Ronan Quinlan

God made the grass, the air and the rain. And the grass, the air and the rain made the Irish. And the Irish turned the grass, the air and the rain back into God.

Sean O'Faolain

A clergyman in Portadown told his congregation, 'If you'd been here this morning to see the empty seats you'd have been ashamed of yourselves for staying away'.

Tony Butler

A lot of people are giving out about the film *The Passion of the Christ*, saying it's anti-Semitic because it makes out that the Jews killed Christ. Well it wasn't the Mexicans!

Dylan Moran

The sexual catalyst to contraception was the Church's problem. I always thought artificial insemination would have been very popular with priests.

Joe O'Toole

It's way beyond ironic that a place called the Holy Land is the location of the fiercest, most deeply-felt hatred in the world.

George Carlin

Dougal: I've heard about all these cults, Ted. People dressing up in black and saying Our Lord's going to come back and save us all.
Ted: No, Dougal, that's us. That's Catholicism.
Dougal: Oh, right.

Fr Ted

When the Pope came to Ireland in September 1979 I was just a little girl. When he was busy telling the young people of Ireland he loved them, I was playing in the house of some Protestant friends.

Róisín Ingle

God is probably a woman. If he was a man he would definitely have put testicles on the inside.

James McKeon

Is Jesus the same as God?

Nora Barnacle

In Ireland in the old days we used to grow priests like potatoes.

Tommy Tiernan

Two guys came knocking at my door once and said, 'We want to talk to you about Jesus.' I said, 'Oh no, what's he done now?'

Kevin McAleer

Jesus was a Palestinian freedom fighter.

Gerry Ryan

W.H. Auden didn't love God; he just fancied him.

Mícheál Mac Liammóir

Did you hear about the priest who was called to a synod by his bishop but wasn't able to make it because he couldn't find a babysitter?

Maureen Potter

We seem to have developed a fast-food attitude to God. We want instant gratification spirituality.

Marian Keyes

Apart from having children, the thing I'm most proud of in my life is ripping up a picture of the Pope on live TV.

Sinéad O'Connor

I'm annoyed by people who say 'God forbid' each time they mention the possibility of an accident or death, especially when they don't believe in God. And people who say 'God rest his soul' following the mention of a dead person, even if they hated the person and don't believe in God.

George Carlin

The Angelus is going downhill, the holy picture of yore replaced by moving pictures of folks who don't necessarily believe in organised religion but who like to pause for a moment's reflection now and again as part of a holistic approach.

Declan Lynch

I don't know why Kate and Gerry McCann went to visit the Pope about the kidnapping of their child. I know he's a Nazi but come on, I can't see he's involved.

Sean Hughes

I can't really believe in a God that could haphazardly intervene during one moment in history, causing air crashes, genocide and famine.

Anthony Clare

I'd prefer to bathe in creosote than to have seen Michael Cleary in the *All Priests' Roadshow*.

John Drennan

The only time kids these days go down on their knees is when they're giving blowjobs.

Fr John Kerrane

The Church in people is more important than people in churches.

Shane Lynch

I went to confession and told the priest I'd committed adultery twice. He said, 'Go out and do it again. This week it's three for five.'

Noel V. Ginnity

When people go to the doctor suffering from depression they give them anti-depressants. One of the side-effects is impotence. This makes you even more depressed. So they give you more anti-depressants. Now you're even more depressed, as well as impotent and totally celibate. The only job that's open for you now is Pope.

Dave Allen

You're closer to God when things aren't going right.

Daniel O'Donnell

Bono was an atheist until he realised he was God.

Kay McLachlan

Like most Irish people, I was born a Catholic. This came as a big shock to my parents, who are both Jewish.

Michael Redmond

Jesus Saves...but Robbie Keane knocks them in from the rebounds.

Graffiti

Catholicism is cheaper than Prozac, but is it good for you?

Marian Keyes

It was reported today that Osama bin Laden has fifty brothers and sisters, which absolutely shocked me. I had no idea he was Catholic.

Conan O'Brien

The main difference between God and Santa Claus is that there really is a Santa Claus.

Dylan Moran

If God didn't want us to gamble he'd never have invented marriage.

Paul Malone

The Christian Brothers are the paramilitary wing of the Catholic Church.

Eamonn Holmes

Why do religious people wear crosses round their necks? If Jesus had been electrocuted, would we wear electric chairs?

Michael Corrigan

I'm not worried about guns in school. You know what I'm waitin' for? Guns in church. That's gonna be a lot of fun.

George Carlin

Is there an afterlife? There should be, because there's an afterbirth.

Kevin McAleer

The first reference to elasticity in the Bible is when Moses tied his ass to a tree and walked ten yards.

Paul Malone

My mother came to the Irish Snooker Masters with me one year but she couldn't bring herself to step inside the auditorium. She spent the whole match sitting in the car with a pair of rosary beads.

Ken Doherty

If God had really been in favour of decimalisation, there would only have been ten disciples.

Sean Gaffney

When I was a kid I thought Jesus spoke with a rural Irish accent. I thought he looked like Jon Bon Jovi, when in reality he probably looked more like Yasser Arafat.

Joe O'Connor

I think it's rather unfair on priests that they're not allowed to get married. I think that if a priest meets another priest and they like one another, they should be allowed to spend their lives together.

Dave Allen

Somehow it has become acceptable to be a Catholic Who Only Believes In Some Bits Of The Religion.

Róisín Ingle

I could never get to grips with the old housewives' tale, 'You can tell a Catholic because their eyes are too close together.'

Gloria Hunniford

Flying is where I always re-discover my faith. All those prayers you learned as a child suddenly come in very useful on take-off, landing, and when turbulence rears its ugly head at 30,000 feet.

Eamonn Holmes

Irish priests are still very much involved with charities in the developing world, but it's a sign of the shift in power that, these days, Ireland's highest-profile missionaries to Africa are Bob Geldof and Bono.

Frank McNally

I support capital punishment. Where would Christianity be if Jesus got eight to ten years, with time off for good behaviour?

James Donovan

The only way you could get me back into the Catholic Church is to have a Chinese Pope. Can you imagine receiving Holy Communion from Him? You'd kneel down and he'd go, 'Are you going to have this here or take it away?'

Dave Allen

Young Irish priests tend to resemble Bing Crosby. When they get older they turn into Barry Fitzgerald.

Frank Gannon

Being an altar boy was my first gig.

Des Bishop

As a teenager I really only went to Mass to see ridey young fellas.

Fiona Looney

And so it came to pass that Jesus sayeth unto Adam, 'Go forth and multiply. And the next day Adam came to Jesus in the Garden of Eden and said, 'Could you tell me, lord, what exactly is a headache?'

Tim McDonald

I'm an atheist, but I'd love to be proved wrong. I'd love to wake up somewhere floating or whatever in a place where nothing happens – a permanent sense of being slightly pissed with your friends.

Roddy Doyle

What's the difference between God and an orthopaedic surgeon? God doesn't think he's an orthopaedic surgeon.

Malachy Smyth

I lost my faith in, of all places, Jerusalem. I was 23. Before that I believed God and His mother were Irish.

Maeve Binchy

The priest at my school used to follow us to dances. He'd come between me and the girl I was dancing with and say, 'You have to keep this far apart' as he indicated his ruler. Presumably he was imagining my penis to be the same size. I always thought he was an incredible optimist.

Dave Allen

All religions are the same. It's basically guilt with different holidays.

Kate Meagher

And God said 'Let there be light' and there was light. But the Electricity Board said He would have to wait until Thursday to be connected.

Spike Milligan

I'm not a lapsed Catholic but rather a collapsed one.

Brendan Gill

It's hard to know if the Church in Ireland will survive or not. If you attend any Sunday Eucharist you're very struck by the absence of young people. We used to say, 'They'll come back when they get married and have children.' I think we're fooling ourselves a bit in that regard.

Bishop Willie Walsh

I always felt sorry for Jesus, being born on Christmas Day and all that. He missed out on a Christmas present.

Michael Redmond

Apparently Saint Patrick used the three-leaved shamrock to explain the Holy Trinity, a three-for-one deal which God had going back then. What history fails to record is that he then used the four-leaved clover to explain how we're a lucky race in case the whole religion thing didn't work out.

Pat Fitzpatrick

One of the consolations of heaven, if we ever find ourselves there, will be that there will be no writers in it.

John McGahern

Like a lot of my generation, I haven't so much turned my back on the Church as sidestepped quietly away. The bookshelves of my friends contain yoga manuals and self-help books now. We're more aware of the coming of Ramadan than Lent.

Jane Rourke

Raising the issue of faith in public dialogue today is a bit like inviting the first wife to the second wedding.

Sean Mullan

A parish priest visited the infants' class of a Catholic school in England and spoke to them about Jesus. Suddenly a child interjected. 'Please, sir,' he said to the priest, 'What channel is he on?'

Gabriel Fitzmaurice

Few people know this, but Pope John 23rd was a member of our family. His real name was Pope John the 23rd Higgins.

Rita Ann Higgins

Ireland hasn't had an officially approved miracle since the Virgin Mary put in a frustratingly brief appearance in Knock in 1897. God ought to see to it immediately.

Terry Eagleton

When you walk on the Liffey boardwalk and look at all those drugged kids with two or three kids with them, you think: What kind of life is this? Maybe we should bring back the Church, bring back hellfire, frighten the life out of them. Nothing else seems to work.

John Banville

Baptism means a better choice of schools. Being a believer doesn't come into it.

Róisín Ingle

The Muslims are the new Irish in England. Give them ten more years and the English will be eating out of their hands. There'll be Muslim theme pubs everywhere, and Osama bin Laden will be Minister for Education.

Patrick Kielty

I didn't believe in reincarnation the last time either.

Shay O'Donoghue

If Adam was an Armagh footballer, he'd still be in Paradise. He would have refused the apple from Eve, seeing as it wasn't on the diet sheet, and settled for a banana instead.

Colin O'Rourke

We've got to start bringing Heaven down to Earth.

Bono

Have you heard about the New Wave Church in California? It has three Commandments and seven Suggestions.

Paul Malone

Isn't there something wrong about a world that believes God is dead and Elvis is still alive?

John B. Keane

You're not an agnostic, Paddy, you're just a fat slob who's too lazy to go to Mass.

Conor Cruise O'Brien

Limerick had a reputation for piety, but we only went into the churches to get in out of the rain.

Frank McCourt

The Church is just a lot of fat Irish bachelors.

Tommy Tiernan

I can't help noticing that nobody blesses themselves any more before getting into the water. I think this has happened since the introduction of lifeguards.

Pat Ingoldsby

I've always been a bit wary of people with strong views and very clear ideas. So many of them don't appear to be very happy. Nobody, so far, has put the fun into fundamentalism.

Tom Doorley

My concept of heaven is having the remote control all to myself.

Brenda Power

The Catholic Church is like the mafia. Once they get you they have you for life.

Frank McCourt

Jesus himself wouldn't stick a Mass in Poland

Tom Galvin

God was satisfied with his work. That is fatal.

Samuel Beckett

Hollywoodland

I told my girlfriend she reminded me of a film star. Lassie.

Brendan O'Carroll

Titanic grossed nearly $2 million, despite Leonardo DiCaprio's woeful Irish accent, and Celine Dion sounding like a demented seagull on the soundtrack.

David Kenny

It's true: our old mistakes come back to haunt us in life. Especially with video.

Peter O'Toole

The premise of *Ghost* is somewhat flawed. It tells us that Patrick Swayze dies, and that this is a bad thing.

Joe Queenan

I said 'fuck' 150 times in *Phone Booth*, and only two were scripted.

Colin Farrell

Roger Moore has two expressions: left eyebrow raised; right eyebrow raised.

Cian Murphy

If I make a good movie they say I'm British and if I make what they think is a bad one they say I'm Irish.

Neil Jordan

I heard Robert Mitchum being interviewed outside his caravan one day during the filming of *Ryan's Daughter*. The reporter asked him, 'What kind of director is David Lean?' The poker-faced Bob replied, 'He is a tall director'.

Niall Toibin

I've never known anyone so sincerely lustful for life nor so disdainful of death.

Lindsay Anderson on Richard Harris

Gene Autry once told me that if John Wayne turned up on a movie set visibly hungover, John Ford made him get into a barrel and stay there till lunchtime.

Hugh Leonard

In Hollywood, brides keep the bouquets and throw away the grooms.

Milo O'Shea

You've just provided me with the makings of one hell of a weekend in Dublin.

Daniel Day-Lewis to those who awarded him an Oscar for *My Left Foot*

Colin Farrell could dangle a baby from a hotel window and we would still cheer.

Róisín Ingle

Every now and then Arnold Schwarzenegger, the man once memorably described as looking like a condom stuffed with walnuts, does something to surprise us. Like acting.

Ian O'Doherty

My friend got a microwave telly. He can watch a three-hour movie in five minutes.

Shaun Connors

At Liz Taylor's last wedding the only people admitted were season ticket holders.

Maureen Potter

People keep asking me if I had sex with Scarlett Johansson. I reply, 'Once you have sex with your co-star, the chemistry goes away.' Anyway, they're more beautiful on screen than in real life. They're all airbrushed.

Jonathan Rhys-Meyers

There was some evidence Jennifer Lopez could act in the early days, but then they started giving her lines and ruined it all.

Brendan O'Connor

A lot of the movies today are what I call McMovies. They're thought up by marketing people for a target audience and they deal with a very limited range of subjects. They're also re-making all the movies they made in Hollywood's Golden Age. It's like they've come to the end of the road. The monster is eating its own tail now and it'll eventually annihilate itself.

Gabriel Byrne

We should be thankful that Ford has allowed the producers of the film to hire an actress (Virginia Madsen) just young enough to be his daughter to be his wife, rather than one young enough to be his grand-daughter. Maybe Hilary Duff was busy.

Donald Clarke on the sixty-three-year-old Harrison Ford in *Firewall*

It was rumoured that several people actually died during the making of *The Ten Commandments*. It was a lot of fun watching out for those bits.

Joe O'Connor

With all the commercialisation, we shouldn't forget the real meaning of Christmas: Bing Crosby's birthday.

Vincent Hanley

I don't think Colin Farrell is good-looking. He just needs a wash.

Katy French

The number of actors trying to get into the Abbey is equalled only by the number trying to get out.

Brian O'Higgins

We were filming John Banville's book *The Newton Letter* for Channel 4. I was playing a deluded historian, Donal McCann a man dying of cancer. He slouched into Jury's Hotel, cap pulled low to shadow the eyes, stomach thrust out like a docker, hands buried in too-large jeans, a racing page underarm. No handshake, just a jerk of the head, the perfunctory acknowledgement of my presence. 'Are you in this effin' pantomime?' he said out of the corner of his mouth.

Gabriel Byrne

What does being an actor mean to me? A bit of gas.

Mick Lally

I've always had the theatre in my veins, but blood might have been better.

Mícheál Mac Liammóir

You can tell within thirty seconds whether somebody has star quality on screen.

Jim Sheridan

Colin Farrell is regarded as a hell-raiser in Los Angeles, but in that town anybody still awake after tea-time can gain such a reputation.

Donald Clarke

Quentin Tarantino has the vocal modulation of a railway station announcer, the expressive power of a fence post, and the charisma of a week-old head of lettuce.

Fintan O'Toole

It's difficult for women over a certain age – about nineteen or twenty – to secure decent roles in Hollywood today.

Donald Clarke

I once interviewed the tight-lipped Robert Mitchum, he of the cowboy 'yups' and 'nopes'. The producer of the show told me he had good news and bad news. 'The good news is we have Mitchum. The bad news is that he's the worst interviewee in the world.'

Gloria Hunniford

Alexander stank like a dead fish in a rubbish bin behind a glue factory.

Eamonn Sweeney

It's the first time I've ever seen lips on an ultrasound.

Conan O'Brien on the pregnant Angelina Jolie

A fella said to me once when I was filming *Bracken*, 'You lot have it aisy, batin' the heads off nettles for a livin','

Gabriel Byrne

Being the artistic director of a theatre isn't such a bad life. I get to consort with people like Al Pacino and Cameron Diaz without having to pay their taxes.

Michael Colgan

Leonardo DiCaprio may be getting sued because he hurled horse manure at the paparazzi while filming his latest movie. In his defence DiCaprio said, 'It wasn't horse manure. It was the script for my latest movie.'

Conan O'Brien

If Robert De Niro gains weight for a role it's called 'artistic dedication'. If I do it's called 'letting yourself go'.

Brenda Fricker

The dialogue in *Troy* isn't so much Greek tragedy as Hollywood tragic.

Tony Clayton-Lea

The Way We Were is close to the top of movies men hate. All men want to look like Robert Redford, but not if they're going to end up with Barbra Streisand.

Joe Queenan

I have only one thing in common with Humphrey Bogart. I once played a scene with Lauren Bacall.

Stephen Rea

Robert De Niro spoke eight words to me when I tried to interview him about his film *Analyse This*. Coming from him, that's practically a novel.

Dave Fanning

I enjoyed *Educating Rita*. What better place than Dublin to make a film about an alcoholic?

Michael Caine

We first became aware of Anne Hathaway in *The Princess Diaries* where her cavernous mouth was overpowered by eyes the size of rowing boats.

Donald Clarke

I refused to believe my father would be denied an Oscar after eight nominations. I refused to believe the Academy would be so callous as to drag a seventy-five-year-old man with a dodgy hip and a career of such matchless quality halfway round the world in order to make him sit through a bum-numbing five hours of light entertainment before humiliating him in front of a television audience of 37 million people.

Kate O'Toole on her father Peter in 2007

I only agreed to appear in a Harry Potter film because my children threatened to disown me if I didn't.

Richard Harris

I see *The Van* as *Thelma and Louise With Chips*.

Roddy Doyle

Before *Ryan's Daughter* the people of Dingle used to eat in and shit out. After it we shat in and ate out!

T.P. O'Connor

When I did *The Commitments* I was staying in Jury's on my own. I just ate chocolate from the fridge because I was too shy to go down to the desk to order anything.

Andrea Corr

My boyfriend won't go to see anything he terms a 'chick flick'. That's any film where the woman talks.

Maura Kennedy

People find it hard to differentiate between your screen character and yourself. When I played the nutter in *Sleeping With the Enemy*, little old ladies were hitting me with their handbags every time I went out for a walk.

Patrick Bergin

No matter how many plays or films I do, a lot of people will still regard me as nothing more than Benjy from *The Riordans*.

Tom Hickey

Quentin Tarantino is a totem for every gawky yoke who ever dreamed of being adored.

Derek O'Connor

Actresses calling themselves actors doesn't make any more sense to me than duchesses calling themselves dukes.

Donal McCann

When I was in the Dublin Shakespeare Society I took part in a production of *Coriolanus* dressed in a black jumper with bell-bottoms. Nobody ever explained to me how Marcus Aufidius happened to be wearing bell-bottoms in Ancient Rome. Nobody knew what anyone else was saying either. All you knew was that when the other guy stopped talking it was your turn to start.

Gabriel Byrne

Getting out of Bond-age was just that for me: a liberation.

Pierce Brosnan

When I was a child we had one of those tellies where you put the ten pence in the slot. It might go just before the end of the programme, but by the time you got the ten pence the programme was over, so you didn't know if the baddie got killed.

Joe Duffy

There's something that always puzzles me about celebrities: Why do people want to become famous and then wear dark sunglasses so that no one will recognise them?

Jason O'Callaghan

How do I remember scripts? Mainly through panic.

Des Cave

I remember my brother saying once, 'I'd like to marry Elizabeth Taylor.' My father said, 'Don't worry, your turn will come.'

Spike Milligan

Colin Farrell is the first and therefore the best bona fide love-'em-and-leave-'em, drink-from-the-bottle, spittin'-and-cursin' goddam movie star this country has ever produced.

Róisín Ingle

I worked with Richard Burton just before he died. I said to him, 'Why did you make so many movies?' I'll never forget what he said, 'When I would wake up on a Monday morning I would say, "I can't bear reality. I'll do another film."'

Gabriel Byrne

Whatever it was that Pierce Brosnan never had, he still hasn't got it.

Phil Carrol

Jaysus, I thought they'd never get him up on that bloody cross!

Deputy film censor Jerome Hegarty on *The Last Temptation of Christ*

LOCATION, LOCATION

By exercising a little caution you can enjoy all the North and West of Dublin have to offer without experiencing anything more troublesome than having to hand over the contents of your handbag to a man wielding a blood-filled syringe.

Ross O'Carroll Kelly

Makeshift fences of crime scene tape and the space age white suits of forensics investigators are providing the contemporary iconography of the Emerald Isle.

Justine McCarthy on Ireland's rising crime-epidemic

L.A. is a place where people order whores like pizza.

Colin Farrell

I told the taxi driver on the way to Helsinki that I was there for five days to shoot a TV show about the place. He said that was about four days too long.

Hector Ó hEochagáin

I'd love to make another film in Ireland but at the moment I can't think of what it would be. I don't want to make one about a thirty-something multiple house-owner.

Neil Jordan in 2007

Before the Celtic Tiger, an Irishman with an inferiority complex was every single one of us potato-eating, self-loathing, pissed Celts with a notion that the Brits might be to blame.

Pat Fitzpatrick

Ireland is now running a deficit of close to 10 billion euro. The problem is how do we find a way of being competitive again. Can you imagine all the Pussycat Moms queuing up beside the Latvians in Lidl for bottles of Muscadet at €2.99 rather than their usual Meursault at €38 from Mitchell's?

David McWilliams

Overheard in Howth pub in the context of rumoured move by Gay and Kathleen to Dublin 4: 'Your man Byrne? Sure he's not a real Dub. Wasn't he born and reared on the south side?'

Gay Byrne

Where we lived was rough. They stole hubcaps from moving cars.

James McKeon

We now live in a vicious little place where a good person is a fool.

Fintan O'Toole

'Dublin,' said the tourist, 'is a very ancient city.' 'It was in the past,' said Cahill, 'but things have changed a lot recently.'

Tony Butler

I once saw a sign on a lift in Dublin that said, 'Please do not use this when it is not working.'

Spike Milligan

We are cannibalising ourselves by educating and hosting the very people who will eventually take our jobs.

David McWilliams on Ireland's Celtic Tiger

In Los Angeles there's a hotline for people in denial. So far no one has called.

George Carlin

One of the reasons I love America is because it will give anyone a hearing even if they have no idea what they're talking about.

Mark Little

The danger with Ireland is that it moved from an unthinking Catholic country to an unthinking materialist one with no stop in between.

David Norris

I'm glad I wasn't born in Italy. I can't speak a word of Italian.

Jack Cruise

This is the first time in my life that Irish people say to me, 'Don't go to England, it's full of terrorists. Stay in Ireland instead. We have no terrorists at all now. They've all become playwrights.'

Dara O'Briain

In Tuam the hire purchase used to be known as '£1 down and £1 when you catch me.'

Jimmy Higgins

Why do people in Ireland always die in alphabetical order?

Shaun Connors

It's estimated that each of us spends one third of our lives in bed – or twice that if your parents are wealthy and you grew up in Killiney.

Paul Howard

I know my level of celebrity in Ireland is small, but all this stuff about how people like Julia Roberts can come here and nobody will go near her – clearly, Julia Roberts doesn't buy fish and chips from the same place I go to. I've been molested in one chip shop in Galway. Somebody shouted out, 'Don't feed the bollocks' while grabbing my testicles. And you can't hit them because they'll take it badly.

Dara O'Briain

I made a phone call to Ireland once. Does that qualify me to play for the national soccer team?

Ken Bolan

Is there life before death?

Seamus Heaney on Northern Ireland during the worst of The Troubles

New Bern in North Carolina is a hole. Empty streets with the crappiest shops you've ever seen, full of stuff that hasn't been fashionable since the thirties. The town is famous, or maybe infamous, for its lost colony: a group of settlers who wandered down here in 1590 and were never seen again. I can put the mystery to rest here and now. It wasn't Injuns or grizzlies that got them. It was boredom.

Hector Ó hEochagáin

It's part of Ireland's national inferiority complex that when someone pays us a compliment we take it as an insult.

Michael Noonan

Growing up in Dublin you expect emigration to happen to you like puberty.

Joe O'Connor

Within a decade most of Dublin will, in fact, consist of housing estates in Wicklow.

Shane Hegarty

Road sign noted in Cork: 'When this sign is under water, the road is closed for traffic'.

Peter Cagney

All my life the mailboat was an object of almost mystic power. England was irrelevant. If China had been next door to Ireland I'd have gone there.

Bob Geldof

As a people, the Irish remind me of what Arnold Bennett said about his neighbours in the Potteries: 'Full of crushed tenderness.'

Con Houlihan

What would you get if you crossed an Irishman with a Jew? A lepracohen.

Colm O'Hara

Navan is the Alabama of Ireland.

Tommy Tiernan

Derry is the only football ground in Europe where the presence of the police would actually provoke a riot rather than prevent one.

Eamonn McCann

Canadians are like Americans except they don't polish their shoes as much.

Conal Gallen

Nobody corrects your pronunciation in Dublin. It's considered bad manners.

Terry Wogan

In Amsterdam if it's fun then it's probably legal.

Hector Ó hEochagáin

Most people in New York don't have cars, so if you want to kill a person you have to take the subway.

George Carlin

I once did four different interviews in four different countries in four different pubs, all called The Dubliner, all in a week.

Roddy Doyle

Do you not feel that Ireland is moored only lightly to the sea-bed, and might be off for the Americas at any moment?

Sebastian Barry

Ireland is the only place in the world where procrastination takes on a sense of urgency.

Dave Allen

I've only been Irish since I moved to England. Back home there didn't seem much point.

Dermot Carmody

When I was in London I lived near an estate where a pit bull was as *de rigueur* as a criminal record. Every time I left my flat to buy a paper the place was overrun with tattooed thugs – and that was just the women.

Marian Keyes

Terry Wogan took on a British accent when he went to England, but it was an Irish British accent. Now you have British people trying to imitate him. An Irishman started by imitating the English and now you have the English trying to imitate an Irishman trying to imitate the English.

Shaun Geoghegan

If you sell your apartment in New York these days, the joke goes, you can't afford to buy a place in Clondalkin.

Fintan O'Toole

The English don't speak unless they have something to say, which is very confusing. I spent a long time trying to chat to people at London bus stops about the weather, the frequency of buses, the state of the country and the future of mankind. In England they don't do that. They thought I was from a home for the bewildered and moved away from me.

Maeve Binchy

I came to Ireland for a fortnight and stayed six years.

Mike Scott

Part of the problem with Ireland is that everything is named after someone. In Dublin there's a railway station called Sydney Parade. For many years I thought Sydney Parade was one of the leaders in the 1916 Rising.

Joe O'Connor

Several Irish motion pictures have portrayed Ballymun as a place where people cohabit with horses, a place where you're likely to meet one in an elevator and pass no remarks.

Declan Lynch

One of the nice things about Irish people is that they never mind you being late for an appointment. Because they're not there either.

Des Bishop

Years ago I would do maybe two suicides a year, if I was unlucky. Now it's not unusual to have two a week.

Belfast undertaker Brendan Brown

I'm a northside snob. I grit my teeth at the nice little Benetton girls who play nicely 'iteside the hice' on fine days in Sandymount or Stillorgan, and warm to bullet-headed little gurriers who mind cars and groom their ponies on the pitted waste ground less than a mile from my front door.

Deirdre Purcell

I'd do anything for Ireland except live there.

Vincent Dowling

The beaches in Spain are brilliant because they're all near the sea.

Conal Gallen

It's often said of Dingle that the next parish is America. I don't like that. Does it imply that the place is the arsehole of Ireland?

Joe O'Toole

The English are a very literal people they think you mean exactly what you say.

Olivia O'Leary

It's said that Finglas is so tough, even the Alsatians walk around in pairs.

Fergal Keane

All good writing is local, and by local I don't differentiate between Ballyfermot and north Roscommon.

John McGahern

South London.
Andy Townsend after being asked what part of Ireland he came from

They never heard of De Valera or Willie Cosgrove in Romania, but they know all about Joe Dolan.

Fergus Muldoon

The reason there are so many Irish jokes is because they have a quaint way with words. Like the patient who hobbled into the surgery's waiting room and said, 'I hope to God the doctor finds something wrong with me because I'd hate to feel like this if I was well.'

George Coote

The Old Irish Dream was of Catholicism, nationalism, community, chastity, the Brits, the six counties, the Irish language, the famine, the underdog, getting a good job in the bank and the glamour of Grace Kelly. The New Irish dream can best be summed up by 'I want the biggest fridge, the best holiday, the newest car, the loudest sound system, the healthiest food, the best yoga posture, the most holistic world-view; the most talked about wedding and the best sex with as many partners, in as many positions, as possible.'

David McWilliams

Growing up I knew I was Irish in the same way I knew I had asthma. Unlike asthma, however, I would never grow out of being Irish.

Frank Gannon

You get a longer sentence in this country for not having a TV licence than you do for a hit-and-run accident.

Leo Lieghio

We're told the streets of Dublin aren't safe any more. Really? I think the streets are very safe indeed. I have a few problems with the people that are on them though.

Jason Byrne

There are parts of the world where Manchester United are the only English words that people know.

Eamon Dunphy

People say to me, 'It must be really tough for you living in Summerhill' and I sort of scratch my head because I would find it much tougher to live in a big Jesuit institution and teach all day long.

Peter McVerry

Everyone is now talking about peace in the North and building a future. I don't mean to worry anyone, but the last thing we built in Belfast went down with Leonardo DiCaprio and Kate Winslet hanging off the back of it.

Patrick Kielty

If the Estonians played any deeper they'd have been in another country.

Mark Lawrenson

German food is so bad, even Hitler was a vegetarian.

Dylan Moran

Canada is the perpetual wallflower that stands on the edge of the hall waiting for someone to come and ask her for a dance.

Kevin Myers

The awful trait the Irish have is the power thing. The fella who thinks he's a policeman when he's just the caretaker, who turns into a Nazi when he's given the responsibility of opening and closing the door.

Pat Shortt

The main reason English people get on well with the Irish is because they're never quite sure from their accents whether they're posh or common.

Terry Wogan

If a Cork astronaut went to the moon, his first words to NASA after looking around would be, 'It's not Cork.'

Tommy Tiernan

Bram Stoker's book about a man with slicked-back hair who dresses in black and sucks blood out of people is believed to be based on his experiences with South Dublin estate agents.

Paul Howard

The health system in Ireland at the moment is like a Third World country.

Brendan Gleeson

The biggest cultural annoyance in Ireland today is supermarket trolleys that won't go straight.

Maria Doyle Kennedy

Ireland is closer to Boston than Berlin.

Mary Harney

Irish people aren't supposed to be speaking English. It's like a brick wall around us. Cursing is the battering ram I use to break through that brick wall.

Tommy Tiernan

I love Dublin because it brings you down to earth. Some years ago I was walking across Fitzwilliam Square when a man shouted at me from across the street, 'I saw ya in *The Courier* and ye were fuckin' brutal.'

Gabriel Byrne

When I was in Mexico for the World Cup I saw a sign in a hotel that said, 'When there are earthquakes, please use the stairs'.

Con Houlihan

I like the Irish but I can't quite understand how the sentence 'I'm from London', in a Dublin pub, tends to be heard as 'I am Oliver Cromwell'.

Jo Brand

Ireland's roundabouts are a kind of vehicular Pamplona.

David Monaghan

I was born in the middle of the Belgian Congo to an English father and a mother from Laois, so I'm a true-blue Dub.

David Norris

Just as a Catholic priest can't be king of England or a woman can't be Pope, so a northsider can't expect to get a job on *AA Roadwatch* due to his or her inability to say 'rayndabayt'.

Pat Fitzpatrick

The city was full of lunatics, people who went into muttering fits on the bus, others who shouted obscenities in automats, lost souls who walked the pavements alone, caught up in imaginary conversations.

Brian Moore

Americans believe in life, liberty and the pursuit of par.

David Robbins

If you don't drink or snort coke or sleep with Colin Farrell, there's nothing to do in Dublin.

Sinéad O'Connor

And then there was the Irishman who went to Pisa and thought the tower was straight.

Dave Allen

The cardinal rule for driving in Ireland is: when in doubt, accelerate.

David Monaghan

Bangkok is like jumping on a spaceship and going to Mars. Only worse.

Ronan Keating

There seems to be a wave of all sorts of Irish performers on British TV at the moment but that could change. Maybe in five years or so British TV will be full of heavy-set Ukrainian farmers.

Tommy Tiernan

Looking back over my nearly thirty years in Tallaght, I often feel like an old pecking hen searching for a soft entry into hard ground.

Eileen Casey

World peace could be a possibility – if it weren't for all those damned foreigners.

Spike Milligan

We Irish are very hard to understand. In one era we turn our heads and say a quiet prayer when we see a Christian Brother give helpless young boys a flogging the likes of which was last seen on African slave ships, and then in another era we elect corrupt politicians as prisoners are tortured in their cells, their human rights smashed to smithereens.

Frances Cahill

In the most recent census, 27% of Monkstown's eighteen- to twenty-five-year-old males listed kite-surfing as their full-time occupation, while 32% listed it as their religion.

Ross O'Carroll Kelly

Don't run out of milk in L.A. The nearest shop is half an hour away.

Deirdre O'Kane

Singapore is a city up its own arse. Can't shout on the street, can't chew gum, can't open the back window of your car…can't understand why anyone would want to go there.

Hector Ó hEochagáin

You know it's summer in Ireland when the rain gets warmer.

Dusty Young

Argentina is a true democracy. Everybody eventually becomes president.

Joe Duffy

70% of Americans don't own a passport. And these people want to take over the world.

Paul Howard

What kind of hellish places do refugees originate from if they perceive Dublin as a better alternative to their homeland?

Donal Ruane

I'm back for another holiday.

Brian Keenan after returning to Beirut in 2007.

Band Aids

I have it on good authority that the manager of one of Ireland's best rock 'n' roll bands, given the choice of the lads being addicted to heroin or golf, said he would marginally prefer if they took to the heroin. 'If they're on smack, you can at least kick them into a taxi and throw them onto a plane, but if they're out golfing you can't even find the bastards.'

Declan Lynch

On the *Just A Minute* quiz one day I asked a contestant 'What star do travellers follow?' The answer I got was 'Joe Dolan!'

Larry Gogan

Sinéad O'Connor acts like she developed her personality in a car accident.

Colin Fraser

The only thing worse than a rock star is a rock star with a conscience.

Bono

The two main motivating factors in my songwriting are revenge and guilt.

Elvis Costello

Am I happy Ronan Keating hasn't done well since leaving me? Of course!

Louis Walsh

Liza Minnelli's last husband was a boiled egg in sunglasses.

Graham Norton on David Gest

Poor old Bob Geldof. Little did he know when he wrote his autobiography *Is That It?* that the title would be so prescient.

Brendan O'Connor

The Provisional IRA have admitted responsibility for the Irish entry in the Eurovision Song Contest this year.

Not the Nine O'Clock News

Elvis Costello is a fat, boring, talentless, four-eyed git.

Shane MacGowan

Great voice, bad rug.

Louis Walsh on Dickie Rock

Dickie Rock has now been in the music business for 142 years.

Ronan Collins

I see Keith Richards has called on young people to stop taking drugs. They have to, Keith. You've taken the lot, you fucker.

Denis Leary

Welshmen sing so much because they don't have locks on their doors.

Hugh Leonard

People often think traditional music is something they should get free in the back room of a pub.

Conor Malone

'I'd like to bump off Dolly Parton'. 'You mean knock off.' 'I know what I mean!'

Seamus O'Leary

To have faith in something, to be happy – that's what most people want, isn't it? With the possible exception of Leonard Cohen.

Marian Keyes

Whenever I told people I was a musician, they used to say 'And do you work as well?'

Donal Lunny

In the old days in Ireland a family's wish was for one of their children to be a priest or a nun. Now it's a pop star.

David Quinn

I've decided to buy Manchester City football club. I'm going to walk in and say, 'You fuck off, you fuck off, you fuck off. And you, make me a cup of tea.'

Noel Gallagher

Nobody knows what Enya's favourite colour is as she's always shrouded in mist.

David Kenny

My first real relationship was with a piano.

Julie Feeney

Alex Higgins is like a manic semi-classical Celtic Jug Band.

Jimmy White

Whenever I get a melody for a new song I ring my Ansaphone and croon it into it before I forget it.

Elvis Costello

Commenting on the Eurovision Song Contest sometimes makes you lose the will to live.

Marty Whelan

I was quite upset that he was better-looking than me.

Dana after being asked how she felt about her namesake Dana International, the transsexual who won Eurovision

The funny thing about music snobs is that most of them don't actually like music.

Des Keogh

When the Capitol started out, they would have cheered even if we played 'Ba Ba Black Sheep'.

Paddy Cole

I love the flute because it's the one instrument in the world where you can feel your own breath.

Michael Flatley

A woman has written a book claiming she was married to Bob Dylan for six years. The marriage wasn't really a secret, but when Dylan told people about it they couldn't understand what he was saying.

Conan O'Brien

Elvis was pretty far gone the first time I saw him. It made sense when women threw their bras at him. He needed them.

Tom Kenny

I look on boy-bands as being commodities like potatoes. They're just better-looking potatoes.

Ronnie Drew

Sure I love Liam. But not as much as I love Pot Noodle.

Noel Gallagher

The high points with the Corrs were very Spinal Tap. Our parents would be dancing round the house in Dundalk as our records went to Number 1, and yet at the same time we'd be doing in-store signings in Detroit to about two people.

Andrea Corr

The only good thing about the eighties was that we got rid of one of the Bee Gees. One down, three to go.

Denis Leary

The older you get, you're just too tired to care about the same things. Rock concerts, I used to camp out for tickets. Now you could tell me Barbra Streisand is playing for free down the street and I'd say, 'How far down the street? Let's just stay here and watch the Discovery Channel. Come on, it's shark week.'

Kathleen Madigan

Music is spiritual. The music business is not.

Van Morrison

Sometimes I feel old. I once asked a girl if she remembered where she was the day Elvis died and she replied, 'I was in my mother'.

Paddy Moloney

Blues music is about having nothing, and then losing it. It's like, 'I don't even have a guitar. I'm strumming my belly button.'

Dylan Moran

Rap is the best poetry being written in America at the moment. At least it rhymes.

Derek Mahon

The atmosphere at Graceland was halfway between Lourdes and Disneyland.

Hector Ó hEochagáin

I enjoyed Eric Clapton more before he went on to be God.

Fran Casey

I love Dolly Parton I don't know why. Maybe it's a subconscious desire to breastfeed.

Graham Norton

My first ambition was to become a jazz musician but I had to keep my parents quiet so I took up medicine.

Ivor Browne

I've always agreed with Séamus Ennis that the only way to play a bodhrán is with a very sharp knife.

Gay Byrne

Mick Jagger once said that he was in the music business for twenty years, but the amount of performing he did in that period only added up to two of those. It's the same with me. Probably 90% of what I do is marketing.

Ronan Keating

I shaved my hair off because somebody confused me with Enya.

Sinéad O'Connor

Ewan McColl said to me, 'Liam, when you start singing a song, you should never know how it's going to end.'

Liam Clancy

The last telegram sent from the *Titanic* has been sold at auction. It said: 'Help! They Won't Stop Playing Celine Dion's Titanic Song.' And then everyone drowned themselves.

Conan O'Brien

Bob Dylan told me I was the best ballad singer he ever heard in his life – but that was only because he stole my girlfriend.

Liam Clancy

Bono to me seems like he's looking for his inner arsehole.

David Feherty

No wonder Bob Geldof is so interested in famine. He's been dining out on 'I Don't Like Mondays' for over twenty years now.

Russell Brand

Why did Ronan Keating cross the road? To get to the middle.

Pádraig Taylor

I had fantastic times with the Dubliners. We had a party that started in 1963 and ended about 1970.

Ronnie Drew

John Lennon took six bullets in the chest, Yoko Ono is standing right next to him. Not one fucking bullet. Explain that to me

Denis Leary

Oasis aren't arrogant, we just think we're the best band in the world.

Noel Gallagher

Why did Michael Jackson skip breakfast? He said he'd grab a little something later.

Conan O'Brien

According to the latest figures Madonna is worth £50 million. And if you include Guy Ritchie's earnings…that's £50 million.

Graham Norton

I've been doing lots of charity gigs lately. Just in case I catch anything in the future.

Noel Gallagher

Genital Persuasion

Sex isn't the answer. Sex is the question. Yes is the answer.

Sean Hughes

I wouldn't fly with Virgin. I'm not interested in anyone that wouldn't go the whole way.

Conal Gallen

A young girl screaming 'Elvis, you're a big ride!' in the Adelphi cinema finally cracked any chance of Catholicism exerting too strong a hold over my sexuality.

Joe Jackson

Virginity is very like a souvenir: priceless to its proprietor but often worth considerably less on the open market.

John B. Keane

Sex education may be a good idea in the schools, but I don't believe the kids should be given homework.

Hal Roach

Sexual excitement, for me, was always linked to pain and separation.

Edna O'Brien

In some places, a seventeen-year-old girl needs a note for being absent from school, but not to get an abortion.

George Carlin

Bill Clinton had sex with Monica Lewinsky in the Oral Office, between two Bushes.

Don Keaveny

If Pete Doherty wasn't shagging a supermodel nobody outside the *NME* would give a shit about him.

Noel Gallagher

An actor once sent me a letter saying, 'I've found a new pill that will solve all your problems. It's a mixture of aphrodisiac and tranquilliser. It makes you want it, but if you don't get it you won't care.'

T.P. McKenna

Condoms are useless because they burst. And your stomach just can't cope with the sudden impact of two kilos of cocaine.

Ardal O'Hanlon

The Flynns couldn't have children, explained Murphy, because sterility was hereditary on both sides of the family.

Tony Butler

Life is a sexually transmitted disease.

Sean Kilroy

A woman said to me, 'Do you know the Balbriggan stud'? I said, 'I *am* the Balbriggan stud.'

Brendan O'Carroll

The boss of Pfizer in Ringaskiddy told me that apparently there was a roaring trade in Viagra at Puck Fair last year – which gives a whole new meaning to the expression 'horny old goat'.

David McWilliams

I got a letter from my mother saying 'Since you left home your father has become a sex maniac. He tries to make love to me any chance he gets. Please excuse the wobbly writing.'

Frank Carson

The first dodgy film I saw was *Emmanuelle*. They made a whole string of those things in the seventies and eighties. Of course it's harmless by today's standards. You'll see racier stuff on *Ros na Rún*.

Hector Ó hEochagáin

The pen is mightier than the sword, but the penis is mightier still.

Joe O'Connor

Sex with no strings attached is a myth. One of the main strings is pregnancy.

David Quinn

A US survey on sexual behaviour has found that most American men think about sex an average of ten times an hour – unless they happen to be called Bill Clinton, in which case they actually *have* sex an average of ten times an hour.

Olaf Tyaransen

I don't feature sex in my books because I've never been to an orgy and I wouldn't know where the arms and legs should be.

Maeve Binchy

I'm all for allowing gay people adopt children, but I don't think they should say things to little boys like 'You throw like a girl' – and mean it as a compliment.

Des Bishop

I have a problem with intimacy. I have to have a tremendous amount of sex with a person before I buy them a drink.

Dylan Moran

Asked to define a nymphomaniac, Alfred Kinsey replied, 'It is simply someone who has more sex than you.'

Eoin Burke-Kennedy

The two most difficult things to portray in a movie are sex and prayer.

Patrick Bergin

Do you think it's possible to recover your sexual dignity if you're just about to get into bed with your lover and she notices a piece of wayward toilet paper sticking out of your bottom?

Michael Redmond

I'm not feeling myself today. They told me it was a sin.

Eddie Maher

I had sex for five hours once, but four and a half was apologising.

Conan O'Brien

If you want your girlfriend to scream while you're having sex, ring her up and tell her.

Martin Tierney

Scientists have discovered that men who natter a lot on mobile phones have lower sperm counts. This raises hopes that they could soon become extinct. At last, peace and quiet on the DART.

Kim Bielenberg

I'm against censorship because it encourages an unhealthy interest in prurience. Perfect proof is, when hard-core porn came in in the States, it bored the hell out of everyone.

Brian Moore

Some people say it's what's on the inside that counts. If that were true of women, *Playboy* would be running centrefolds of brain tissues and gall bladders.

Christy Murphy

I met a male porn star in the San Fernando Valley and, get this, he's married. Can you imagine that in Ireland? Back from a hard day at the orifice; and the wife asks you how was the traffic and did you ride anyone nice today.

Hector Ó hEochagáin

Promiscuity is even more boring than fish and chips.

Edna O'Brien

The last time I had sex, it was so good even the neighbours had a cigarette.

Des Bishop

Nothing separates a girl from her knickers faster than a guy with a Northern accent.

Pat Fitzpatrick

Circumcision is no skin off my nose.

Shaun Connors

They used to say that if you lost your virginity in Cork, someone would be sure to find it and bring it back to your mother.

Maeve Binchy

We were so poor that if we woke up on Christmas morning without an erection, we had nothing to play with.

Frank McCourt

Sex before marriage is a good idea – mainly because there's so little after it.

Brendan O'Carroll

Jane Russell increased the masturbation rate in Rathmines to the point where it went off the graph when I was young.

Lee Dunne

I was once propositioned by an elderly plumber of about seventy, with emphysema, who offered me two and sixpence for a look at my privates.

Gabriel Byrne

What I have always liked about the Irish Republic is that it is, of all the societies I know, the least sexy.

Donald Davie

My girlfriend is a real sex object. Every time I ask her for sex she objects.

Frank Kelly

Trying to end prostitution by criminalising the prostitutes is like trying to end poverty by making it criminal to be poor.

Mary Harney

I don't like kids so I spray-painted 'Paedophile' all over my front wall. They broke all the windows, but it was worth it.

Sean Hughes

The biggest mistake I made in my early days with Boyzone was telling a reporter that I was a virgin.

Ronan Keating

I wouldn't be surprised to see even a turnip described as sexy in today's world so that it will sell.

Angela McNamara

Before *Sex and the City* I thought a 'Brazilian' was a footballer.

David McWilliams

A Jesuit at Belvedere once asked his religion class what they thought about sex on the television. One boy replied, 'I don't know about you, Father, but I find it very uncomfortable.'

Tom Doorley

A poll showed 14% of men have received oral sex while driving. They must be the same 14% who are deathly afraid of speed bumps.

Conan O'Brien

The Blessed Virgin conceived without sinning. I'd like to sin without conceiving.

Stephen Behan

Sir Christopher Dilke kept his wife in one part of a very big bed and his mistress in another, and neither ever knew the other was there.

Tony O'Reilly

Adam came first. But then men usually do.

Cliodhna Kenny

When a masochist brings someone home from the bar, does he say, 'Excuse me for a moment, I'm going to slip into something uncomfortable.'

George Carlin

The world dictates that heteros make love, while gays have sex.

Boy George

Did you hear about the girl who went home and told her mother she was pregnant and her mother said, 'Are you sure it's yours?'

Dennis Taylor

A woman once told me she listened to me through five pregnancies. There are very few fellas on the wireless who were listened to through five pregnancies. And had nothing to do with any of them.

Gay Byrne

A child is too old to breastfeed when he can unhook Mommy's bra with one hand.

Anthony Clark

The secret of sex is not to take it seriously.

John B. Keane

Delaney was asked if he talked to his wife while he was making love. 'Only if there's a phone handy,' he said.

Shaun Connors

I'm happy to say I've never paid for sex in my life. Which meant a lot of prostitutes I've been with are pretty pissed off.

Sean Hughes

I feel sorry for homeless gay people. They have no closet to come out of

George Carlin

The only people I knew in London were gay. I became a fag-hag by default.

Marian Keyes

Kingsley Amis once recommended sex as a cure for a hangover. This makes sense because if I thought Kingsley Amis was going to make love to me I'd certainly avoid getting drunk

.

Joe O'Connor

This Sporting Life

IRFU: the most damning prefix in Irish life.

Kevin Myers

I never play cricket. It requires one to assume such indecent postures.

Oscar Wilde

Martin O'Neill, standing, hands on hips, stroking his chin.

Mike Ingham

I don't really miss boxing since I retired. I miss the *craic* in the gym, but not being smacked in the mouth every day.

Barry McGuigan

Another fine mess, Stan.

Garry Doyle on Steve Staunton after Ireland failed to beat Cyprus during our Euro 2008 qualifier

While the state of British sport may be mostly serious but never hopeless, the state of Irish sport, although usually hopeless, is never serious.

Former IRFU president Noel Henderson

I only ever hit Roy Keane once. He got up, so I couldn't have hit him very hard.

Brian Clough

It looks like there's a bit of a schmozzle in the parallelogram.

Mícheál O'Hehir

He's now so unemployable the only job he'll get is temping in an office in Sandyford.

Aoibhinn O'Súilleabháin after Staunton was sacked as Ireland's manager

When we entered the parlour the defendant was naked and in an aroused state. When asked the reason for his presence at the establishment, he said he was being treated for a sporting injury.

Garda who raided a massage parlour in Dublin

If I ever insinuate that I'm returning to county management, I will tell my wife to have me shot straight away.

Ger Loughnane

I can't tell you what a relief it was to me when the Rebecca Loos episode showed the Beckhams' marriage isn't without its patchy moments. Now whenever I see Victoria clutch David, I know she's not expressing affection. She's holding on for all she's worth.

Martina Devlin

The pressures in snooker can give you brain damage. Maybe that's why I married a psychiatrist.

Ken Doherty

What's wrong with drugs in sport? If someone wants to run the 100 metres in half a second, let him. It's only a programme on the telly. What I want to see is him trying to slow down as he gets to the bendy bit.

Tommy Tiernan

I'm out at the moment, but should you be the chairman of Barcelona, AC Milan or Real Madrid, I'll get straight back to you.

Joe Kinnear's answerphone message

The nicest thing about looking at a picture of a 1950s baseball park is that the only people wearing baseball caps are the players.

George Carlin

Angling is like fishing, but for middle class people.

Paul Howard

Robbie Keane can't hit a barn door at the moment.

Steve Staunton after Ireland drew with Cyprus in a Euro 2008 qualifier in October 2007

An auld fella said to me one day, 'When I was your age, hurlin' was dangerous and sex was safe.'

Pat Shortt

Those of us on the soccer beat have had the misfortune to cover what I call yellowpack managers.

Eamon Dunphy

Why doesn't Sonia O'Sullivan leave the house a bit earlier and then she wouldn't have to run so fast?

Ray D'Arcy

A training session in rugby in the 1970s consisted of running around Barry McGann twice.

Tony O'Reilly

If Offaly ever win the National League again it will be the greatest accident since the Titanic.

Paul O'Kelly

I love Cork so much that if I caught one of their hurlers in bed with my missus I'd tiptoe downstairs and make him a cup of tea.

Joe Lynch

Being a Kerry manager is probably the hardest job in the world because Kerry people, I'd say, are the roughest type of fucking animals you could ever deal with.

Páidí Ó Sé

People think Ireland is divided into orange and green. Actually the predominant colour is red – Man United red.

Eamonn Holmes

The reason boxers don't have sex the night before a fight is because they usually don't fancy each other.

Jimmy Carr

There were a number of reasons my sporting career was cut short. Lack of time, a disinclination to practise...and the fact that I was totally and utterly crap.

Michael O'Driscoll

I have a suggestion for Roman Abramovich. Use your money to buy all the best players in the world for Chelsea. Then buy all the other teams in England and the rest of Europe. And make sure they only have shite players. You'll win everything. Then, hopefully you'll shag off back to the arse-end of Russia or wherever it is you're from.

Paddy Murray after Abramovich dismissed Jose Mourinho from Chelsea in 2007

Oliver Saint John Gogarty won a bronze medal at the Olympics in 1924 for poetry. This was back in the days when Ireland won medals and didn't have to give them back a few weeks later.

Ross O'Carroll Kelly

When the going gets rough, the Irish get singing. If we could only have sung our victory we'd have won.

Lise Hand after Ireland's 25–3 hammering by France in the Rugby World Cup in 2007

Jean Tigana has spent the entire first half inside Liam Brady's shorts.

Jimmy Magee

Kevin Kilbane's head is better than his feet. If only he had three heads, one on the end of each leg.

Eamon Dunphy

Not long ago in Ireland, admitting that you liked cricket was, well, just not cricket.

Cormac Bourke

When I was a child we watched many football games on the radio.

Con Houlihan

I didn't think he'd miss it again on the action replay.

Sil Fox

A player as talented as David Beckham comes with a lot of baggage – most of it Louis Vuitton.

Joe O'Connor

The motto of Irish rugby has always been 'Kick ahead'. Any head.

Fergus Slattery

A Kerry footballer with an inferiority complex is one who thinks he's just as good as everyone else.

John B. Keane

Hurling and sex are the only two things you can enjoy without being good at them.

Jimmy Deane

Jack Charlton's philosophy of soccer was, 'If plan A fails, try Plan A'.

Mark Lawrenson

I love football. I just don't like it.

John Maughan

The last time we played England we beat them one–all.

Jim Sheridan in 1994

When Meath played Mayo in the All-Ireland, 31 counties wanted Mayo to win.

Sean Boylan

If I had been born ugly, you'd never have heard of Pele.

George Best

There are very few pretty All-Irelands.

Sean Boylan

Green is associated with many tragedies in Ireland. 1798, for instance, and the Famine, and the current rugby team.

Frank McNally

I always hated sports at school. The only reason I played netball was because I was so tall I only had to drop the ball into the net. And we got tea and buns after the games when we travelled to other schools.

Maeve Binchy

It used to be joked that, in Northern Ireland, a GAA player might escape censure for playing rugby by arguing that it was the only way he could legally assault a policeman.

Frank McNally

Steve Staunton's honeymoon as manager of Ireland lasted about as long as one of Britney Spears's marriages.

Kevin Palmer

I had a hurley in my hand by the time I was fourteen months old.

Justin McCarthy

It is difficult to play well against poor opposition, but San Marino tried their best.

Colman O'Neill on Ireland's narrow victory over San Marino in the European Cup qualifying match in 2007

San Marino play like men who expect to encounter visa problems if they approach the halfway line.

Tom Humphries

They're calling me Valdarama, but I feel more like Val Doonican.

Andy Townsend after dyeing his hair blonde for the 1994 World Cup

If I'm speaking to aspiring young commentators I say to them, 'There is only one crime: silence.'

Mícheál Ó Muircheartaigh

My problem with Paul McGrath was whether to give him appearance money or disappearance money.

Ron Atkinson

When I pick a team I don't pick the eleven best, I pick the best eleven.

Brian Kerr

Peter Finch won an Oscar for *Network*, in which he played a newscaster who promised to die on air. Ideally that's how I'd like to go, maybe at full-time during a Six Nations broadcast. Preferably after I've offered my analysis of the match.

George Hook

What do the Derry football team and Frank Bruno have in common? They're both out after round one.

Internet joke

Pat Fox has the ball on his hurl now and he's motoring well, but here comes Joe Rabbitte hot on his tail. I've seen it all now – a rabbit chasing a fox around Croke Park.

Mícheál Ó Muircheartaigh

I don't like rugby and I work for *The Irish Times*. It's like being a day trader and working for *Pravda*.

Tom Humphries

The best excuse I ever got from a player who was late for training was the one who told me a wheel fell off his mobile home.

Eugene McGee

When Roger Bannister broke the four-minute mile record, I remember thinking with my childish logic that from now on it would only take me eight minutes to walk the two miles to school.

Gloria Hunniford

I sometimes think I must be the only person in Britain who has featured on the front, centre and back pages of a daily newspaper – all on the same day.

George Best

I'm always suspicious of games like hurling where you're the only ones that play it.

Jack Charlton

Ever since I was appointed manager of Sunderland I've been walking around the place looking like I've got a coat hanger in my mouth.

Mick McCarthy

I don't mind someone not being interested in sport; the annoying aspect is that such people tend to boast about their indifference.

Con Houlihan

When men are at a football stadium they're there to watch the game. You could prance half-naked across the pitch and the only response you'll get from the menfolk in the stalls is 'Get off'. Not, you'll notice, 'Get 'em off'.

Anne Marie Scanlon

The only things I always have in my wallet are the Saint Francis Xavier novena of grace and the Man United fixtures list.

Bertie Ahern

90% of my money went on women, fast cars and booze. The rest I wasted.

George Best

Danny Blanchflower was a lovely lad, even though he was Irish.

John Charles

Lou Gehrig died of Lou Gehrig's disease. How did he not see it coming?

Denis Leary

The proliferation of soccer on this island is about the best thing that happened to us since the arrival of the potato.

Con Houlihan

George Best's whole life was a suicide note.

Michael Parkinson

How many soccer players does it take to change a light bulb? Eleven. One to stick it in and ten to hug and kiss him afterwards.

Tom Humphries

Great managers have to be ugly and swear a lot.

George Best

People think I'm too nice, but I'm not going to be a nasty bastard just so someone is going to think better of me for it.

Ken Doherty

Pope John Paul II was a soccer goalie in his youth. So even as a young man he tried to stop people from scoring.

Conan O'Brien

The Irish play soccer, rugby and some cricket as well as hurling and Gaelic football. Other sports include turning signposts around in the countryside to confuse tourists, and a game played by bus drivers, which consists in four buses which were supposed to have arrived at ten minute intervals, holding back for an hour and then all arriving together.

Terry Eagleton

In much the same way as Zulu warrior was obliged to kill a lion in order to assume warrior status, it was considered manly to draw the occasional clout at a referee.

John B. Keane

Today is the first Sunday after Pentecost, or the third Sunday after Punchestown.

Fr Sean Breen

The GAA has grounds that are state of the art, and an administration that's state of the Ark.

Ger Loughnane

David Beckham is the Anna Kournikova of football. How can someone who doesn't use his left foot, who doesn't know how to head the ball, doesn't tackle and doesn't score many goals, be considered a great player?

George Best

Anyone who uses the word 'quintessentially' in a half-time talk is talking crap.

Mick McCarthy

The fools. They've scored too early.

Eamonn Sweeney on a 1999 game of Gaelic football in which Sligo scored first and then lost

Alex Higgins uses running side, reverse side, back side, any sort of side. The only side he hasn't attempted yet is suicide.

Ray Reardon

Colin Meads is the kind of player you expect to see emerging from a ruck with the remains of a jockstrap between his teeth.

Tom O'Reilly

The 21st goal was offside.

Brian Kerr after his Under-21 side won a match by 22 goals to nil

Victory has a thousand fathers but defeat is an orphan.

Sean Boylan

I had no interest in going straight into football management after my playing career ended. My plan was to chill out for a few years and spend time with my family, but they got fed up with me. My wife dropped me off at the stadium.

Roy Keane

Vinnie Jones would bawl like a baby if he ever came up against Brian Mullins, Brian McGilligan or Brian Corcoran. And that's just three Brians who spring to mind.

Tom Humphries

Steve Davis is so laid back he used to take Valium as a stimulant.

Dennis Taylor

What have Sinn Féin and Tyrone got in common? Sinn Féin have a better chance of seeing an All-Ireland.

Colin O'Rourke

They think we're just a bunch of ignorant paddies from the bog. Let's not disappoint them.

Stewart McKinney before a rugby match against England

Tony Ward is the most important rugby player in Ireland. His legs are more important to his country than Marlene Dietrich's were to the film industry.

C.M.H. Gibson

So that's what you look like. I've played against you three times and all I've ever seen is your arse.

Welsh international Graham Williams to George Best after Best's international debut for Northern Ireland in 1964

Are you a croque, monsieur?

Risteard Cooper to Irish rugby coach Eddie O'Sullivan after our World Cup nightmare in September 2007

We always called Dennis Taylor The Lobster because he went so red in the face any time he was losing a game.

Ronnie O'Sullivan

An old teacher of mine used to tell a story about asking an old footballer in Kerry what it meant to have an All-Ireland medal. There was a pause and finally an answer: 'Yerra, I'd have five of them and I suppose there'd be a small bit more thought of me than a man who'd only have the four.'

Tom Humphries

There's one immutable law of snooker: Always bet against Jimmy White.

Ray McAnally

We're a nation of fat drunk people.

Mick O'Dwyer

It's always the same when I go to bed with women. When they're taking off their clothes they say, 'I hope you don't think I'm doing this just because you're George Best.'

George Best

There are some people on the FAI that I wouldn't allow mind the corner shop.

Brian Kerr

Steve Staunton was launched by John Delaney, who we now realise was only doing so because his wife and children were being held at gunpoint.

Tom Humphries in sardonic mood following Delaney's distancing himself from the beleaguered Staunton

Himself likes football. That's because he's a man. I don't like football. That's because I'm a woman. Although I pretend I love it. That's because I'm a *modern* woman.

Marian Keyes

I'm not an outdoorsy type. If I was offered a choice between whitewater rafting and being savaged by a rabid dog, I'd be likely to tick the box marked 'Dog'.

Marian Keyes

Battles With the Bottle

Alex Higgins never drinks unless he's alone or with somebody.

Dennis Taylor

I'm not saying the pub I drink in is rough, but they have a pig on the counter for an air freshener.

Sil Fox

The Irish tend not to say 'He was drunk' but 'Drink had been taken'. This is a pleasant way of implying that you were drunk but didn't do it yourself.

Terry Eagleton

I'm Irish and Dutch. Which means my idea of a good time is to get drunk and drive my car into a windmill.

Kris McGaha

Never refuse wine. It is an odd but universally held opinion that anyone who doesn't drink it must be an alcoholic.

P.J. O'Rourke

When I think of the hardship involved in only having seven hours to drink on a Sunday my soul shudders.

Kevin O'Higgins

I'm not a writer with a drinking problem. I'm a drinker with a writing problem.

Brendan Behan

Someone threw a petrol bomb at Alex Higgins the last time he was in Belfast…and he drank it.

Frank Carson

Shane MacGowan is off the drink now. He just drinks wine.

Frank Skinner

The last time she was in Dublin I brought her to Mulligan's in Poolbeg Street and she loved it. I don't take her to The Summit in Howth because too many of my ex-flings still drink there.

Stuart Townsend on his long-time partner Charlize Theron

You can write with a hangover. That's why so many writers are alcoholics.

Neil Jordan

Foxrock is the only village in Ireland without pubs as they're considered more working class than dying for Ireland.

Paul Howard

The first time a man told me he was going to 'crack a cold one' I thought he was making a reference to necrophilia.

Michael Mee

If you put a bottle of vodka in one hand and your kids in the other, the alcoholic will probably go for the vodka.

Paul McGrath

When I drank, there was nothing else in my world except drink. And now that I don't drink, there's nothing in my world except not drinking.

Declan Lynch

I once told a doctor how much I was drinking and he said to me, 'Have you thought about getting help?' 'No,' I replied, 'I can drink it all by myself.'

David Feherty

Two Irishmen walk into a bar and ask for a drink. The barman says, 'Sorry, we're closed.' To which one of the Irishmen replies 'How did we get in then?'

Dave Allen

Alcoholism is the loneliest disease on Earth.

Fergal Keane

I became an actor because I didn't want to be Malachy McCourt, and I became an alcoholic because I didn't want to be Malachy McCourt.

Malachy McCourt

I always thought that out-drinking men twice my size was sexy.

Marian Keyes

If it was raining champagne, a real Dub would stay at home.

David Kenny

The French drink for cuisine, the Irish for...lining.

Michael Mee

The main difference between a straight man and a bisexual is three and a half pints of lager.

Graham Norton

I'd hate to be an alcoholic with Alzheimer's. Imagine needing a drink and forgetting where you put it.

George Carlin

There's no smoke to be found in the pubs now because it's not right to have punters eating the carvery lunch in a smoky environment. Funny, it never occurred to anyone that maybe it wasn't right to have poor auld fellas trying to drink and smoke with a fucking carvery lunch going on all around them.

Declan Lynch

Alcoholics often convince themselves they can't write without alcohol. It's another excuse to drink.

Marian Keyes

A man went to a doctor. The doctor said, 'I can find nothing wrong with you. It must be the drink.' 'It's all right,' the man said, 'I'll come back when you're sober.'

Shaun Connors

I once drank poteen laced with brandy. I went on fire and had to be put out with Beamish.

Joe McCarthy

I made a new year's resolution to give up boozing once. But I was drunk at the time.

Richard Harris

Years ago I had a friend who used to send a bunch of carnations with a note of apology after every drunken gathering. Someone once asked him if he could send the flowers before the next party as it would save the hostess from having to buy any.

Maeve Binchy

Spirits are a problem when you can't get hold of them, and an even bigger problem when you can.

Shane MacGowan

You can get gay anything now: gay tea, gay coffee, gay lager. The last one is like straight lager except it goes down easier.

Graham Norton

Real Dublin drinkers never get drunk. The word 'drunk' on its own isn't considered to be flexible enough to describe the level of inebriation attained by the imbiber. They get stewed, tipsy, plastered, blotto, stocious, paralytic, jarred, mouldy, well-oiled, maggoty, well-on, fluthered, pickled, drunk as a skunk, under the weather, creased, three sheets in the wind, twisted, locked or rat-arsed.

David Kenny

The man was a secular version of the Immaculate Conception. He became an alcoholic without ever buying a drink.

Niall Toibin

I was in favour of the cigarette ban in pubs. Now I'm a member of the select generation who had the supreme pleasure of going into the pub jacks for a pee and splitting the butt-end of a fag in half in the urinal.

Sean Hughes

The only difference between a wedding and a funeral in Ireland is there's one less drunk.

Michael Ross

Once I started drinking I couldn't stop. And once I stopped, I couldn't stay stopped.

Marian Keyes

One in four Irish people never touch a drink, which makes the statistical achievements of the rest of them all the more impressive.

Frank McNally

Being an alcoholic like me makes it difficult to be in hotel rooms with mini-bottles of booze in the fridge. I've been in staring matches with mini-bars. And mini-bars seldom blink.

David Feherty

I fell down the stairs with two large glasses of whiskey but I didn't spill any. I managed to keep my mouth shut.

Brendan Grace

By law, whether you're hungry or not, you have to stop for chips on the way home from an Irish pub.

Ardal O'Hanlon

The extent of George Best's drinking was most revealed when his new liver asked for a free transfer to Paul Gascoigne.

Dead Ringers

Turns of Phrase

There's no time like the present for postponing what we don't want to do.

Joe Daly

Why is 'abbreviation' such a big word?

Ed Byrne

Outside every thin woman there's a fat man trying to get in.

Seán Mac Réamoinn

The main trouble with lipstick is that it doesn't.

Maureen Potter

Always eschew obfuscation.

Flann O'Brien

Boxers make money hand over fist.

Noel Andrews

He who laughs last didn't get the joke.

Jack Cruise

God loves a trier, but he hates a chancer.

Donal Ruane

One thing doesn't always lead to another. Sometimes one thing leads to the same thing. Ask an addict.

George Carlin

Mary was a maniakleptic. She used to walk into shops and leave things.

Shaun Connors

I'm living proof that dieting makes you fat.

Marian Keyes

There was method in their sanity.

Con Houlihan

God never closes a door but he catches your fingers in it.

Christy Kenneally

The plain shall inherit the earth.

Graham Norton

Only dead fish go with the flow.

Roy Keane

The great BBC maxim is: if it ain't broke, break it.

Terry Wogan

My old friend Senator Harris seems to have an endless penchant for Eoghan goals.

Con Houlihan

I've always been a scrubber.
  Boy George on the community service he was sentenced to in 2006

Throwing acid is wrong. In some people's eyes.

Jimmy Carr

I have a problem with people who say 'No problem'.

George Carlin

They say a woman's work is never done. Maybe if they organised themselves a bit better…

Jimmy Carr

Finnegan said with despair he was hoarse listening to his wife.

Tony Butler

My heart was pounding and I was feeling as sick as the proverbial donkey.

Mick McCarthy

Should old acquaintance be forgot and never brought to mind? Take it from me, the short answer is *yes*!

Joe O'Connor

The funny thing about legs is that the bottom is at the top.

Danny Cummins

Rome wasn't built in a day – but then I wasn't on that job.

Brian Behan

'Don't make the same mistake twice' seems to indicate three mistakes.

George Carlin

The truth may set you free, but first it will make you miserable.

Damien Scallon

McCarthy will have to replace Cascarino because he's quickly running out of legs.

Mark Lawrenson

'Not by bread alone doth man live,' said Callaghan as he sliced the pig's cheek, 'but by butter and beer and sausages.'

John B. Keane

Bertie Ahern killed three birds with a rolling stone when he refused to play 'smokes and daggers' with the issue of his pay increase.

Frank McNally

Forgive your enemies, but remember their names.

John F. Kennedy

Englishman: 'And is this your most charming wife?'
Irishman: 'No, it's the only one I've got.'

Peter Cagney

Mícheál Mac Liammóir is up to his hilt in Edwards.

Kevin Dwyer

On a rough passage to the Aran Islands, Colm groaned that the hope of dying was the only thing that kept him alive.

Tony Butler

Once bitten, twice inoculated.

Joe Carroll

'Where were you born?'
'Kilcock.'
'What part?'
'All of me.'

James McKeon

Give a man a fish and you feed him for a day. Give him a fishing rod and you can shag his wife all day long.

Sean Killeen

Absence makes the heart go wander.

Bill Kelly

When in Rome, stay there.

John Huston

Michael Flatley can dance at 35 beats per second. Only his bank account ticks up faster.

Sunday Telegraph

Nobody is going to be hanged on the guillotine.

Bertie Ahern

Familiarity breeds content.

Sam McAughtry

He caught that with the outside of his instep.

George Hamilton

I was born at home because I wanted to be near my mother.

Joe Duffy

Charlie Haughey tried to transform Temple Bar into Ireland's West Bank.

Bertie Ahern

It's slightly alarming the way Manchester United decapitated against Stuttgart.

Mark Lawrenson

Is the Pope a Catholic? Does Dolly Parton sleep on her back?

Barry Egan

I'd rather play in front of a full house than an empty crowd.

Johnny Giles

I worry, therefore I am.

Marian Keyes

Many are called, but few get up.

Maureen Potter

Enough is never enough when it comes to poetry.

Seamus Heaney

In the spring a young man's fancy turns to things he's already been thinking about all winter.

Gene Fitzpatrick

All work and no play makes Jack's wife a rich widow.

Tom McDermott

We're on the crest of a slump.

Jack Charlton

Gay Mitchell is the evil of two lessers.

Michael McDowell

Success is relative. The more success, the more relatives.

Jason Byrne

Home is where the hurt is.

Kitty Holland

My mother told me never to worry about sticks and bones.

Bertie Ahern

The Write Stuff

A man once bought a packet of condoms in a shop because he was too embarrassed to buy my autobiography.

Terry Wogan

A good way to write a novel is to go into a pub, sit down and listen.

Maeve Binchy

The two worst experiences for a writer are to see books so good they dishearten him, or abysmal ones selling better than his own.

John Broderick

The true artist is a mad man who tries to appear sane: the phoney one a sane man trying to appear mad.

Bryan MacMahon

The privilege of being a publisher is being able to lift the phone and talk to anybody you want to. People are always glad to hear from a publisher.

Antony Farrell

All good writing is swimming under water and holding your breath.

F. Scott Fitzgerald

In most newspapers you have to read between the lines, but in the *Sunday World* you have to read between the legs.

Fr Brian D'Arcy

Playwrights only puts down what we says, and then charges us to hear it.

Denis Murphy

I write from my bed. So far it's worked out nicely, especially since I've started turning myself regularly to avoid bedsores.

Marian Keyes

Life is hard enough without having to read Samuel Beckett.

Brian Behan

My father never let the facts get in the way of a good story.

Benedict Kiely

I like something Rilke said: 'There are certain books that must long for the death of their author so that they can assume their lives.'

John McGahern

Even dead Irish poets posed some sort of threat to Paddy Kavanagh.

Anthony Cronin

I wrote one of my books rocking a pram with one hand and typing with the other.

Anne Enright

Monkstown has always been a beacon for arty types. Go for a walk along the seafront and chances are you'll be accosted by a man in an Aran sweater with smelly hair, selling a book of his poetry.

Ross O'Carroll Kelly

Evelyn Waugh was a misanthrope, but could be excused because he never got over having been christened with a girl's name. If a man called Evelyn is reading this he will probably hit me with his hockey stick.

Hugh Leonard

Writing is like getting married. One should never commit oneself until one is amazed at one's luck.

Iris Murdoch

There are passages of *Ulysses* that can be read only in the toilet if one wants to extract the full flavour from them.

Henry Miller

I'm a patient man. I once spent six months on a paragraph trying to get it right. I take my lead from Arnold Schoenberg. He was once informed that a violin concerto he wrote would require a soloist with six fingers to play it. He replied, 'I can wait.'

John Banville

I don't need yoga, valium or any other relaxant. When necessary, I recite the first few verses of *Gray's Elegy*.

Mike Murphy

A book isn't finished when a writer writes 'The End'. It's only finished when it's read. For every reader it's a different book.

John McGahern

The Irish Times – that last bastion of the semi-colon.

Con Houlihan

Cats know with absolute certainty which part of the newspaper you're trying to read. This is the only place in the whole house where they decide to sit.

Pat Ingoldsby

The only people who have trouble with poetry are the people who link it with 'literature'. It's much more akin to mountain-walking or dancing with yourself at 2 am.

Theo Dorgan

My favourite Irish joke concerns the worker on the building site who's asked if he knows the difference between a joist and a girder. 'Of course I do,' he says, 'Joist is the man who wrote *Ulysses* and girder wrote *Faust.*'

Mary Kenny

Brendan Behan read everything he could as a child. One day his father found him up in bed reading the back of a tram ticket he'd picked up off the floor.

Ulick O'Connor

I could not have gone on through the awful wretched mess of life without having left a stain upon the silence.

Samuel Beckett

The intensity of a short story would be intolerable in a novel.

John McGahern

One of the great things about being a writer is the extent to which it allows us to re-invent ourselves. It's like being in a witness-protection programme.

Paul Muldoon

Like everything else in Ireland, poetry is contentious. There is always an occasion of outrage.

Denis Donoghue

During my time at *The Mirror* I worked under John Kearns and Neil Leslie. Both of them taught me a great deal about tabloid newspapers, like to use the word 'spine-chilling' frequently.

Jason O'Callaghan

The short poem sells just as well as the long one. That is to say, it usually doesn't sell at all.

Frank McNally

Poetry sections are usually put in the back of bookshops, like pornography.

Desmond Clarke

One should not look to poets for handy hints. W.B. Yeats had trouble walking properly, let alone boiling an egg without cracking it.

Craig Brown

Boots for the Footless is a fromp: a cross between a farce and a romp.

Alan Titley

Once you've put one of Henry James' books down you simply cannot pick it up again.

Oscar Wilde

When a writer has the feeling that he can't do it any more he descends into hell.

Edna O'Brien

When John McGahern died, he was like a secular saint. That guy taught me in Belgrove. But when he died he was almost like Padre Pio.

Neil Jordan

Mr Joyce tries to put everything in. I try to leave everything out.

Samuel Beckett

I was an English teacher for 14 years. I spent hours trying to convince the pupils that Yeats wasn't an eejit about Maud Gonne MacBride. They'd go, 'Sir, why didn't he just ask her to go out with him?'

Roddy Doyle

If you're seriously bent on becoming a real Dublin writer it's important to make an enemy as soon as you can or nobody will take you seriously.

David Kenny

Poets should never marry.

Maud Gonne MacBride

For my friends a party means fun and glamour. For me it means research.

Marissa Mackle

One critic dismissed my work as 'Champagne and shopping' and I thought: What book had he read? I'm more 'Hot chocolate and Maltesers'.

Patricia Scanlan

I don't write tragedies.

John B. Keane after being asked if he would write a play on Páidí Ó Sé's time as manager of Kerry

An author at the Frankfurt Book Fair is basically an inconvenience.

Joe O'Connor

The Irish bottle up their grievances rather than deal with them. And when they have enough saved up they either go mad or write a book.

Frank McNally

Chicklit grows like topseed.

Declan Kiberd

Only a fool would write out of happiness.

John McGahern

Writing poetry is my way of taking photographs of myself.

Gabriel Byrne

When Keats was my age he had been dead for eleven years. This clearly gave him an unfair advantage with the critics.

Joe O'Connor

Young writers today are smothered by the toxic environment of celebrity.

Eavan Boland

A woman looked at a book of mine one day and said 'I could do that'. 'Maybe you could,' I replied, 'but I *did* it.'

Maeve Binchy

James Joyce would have liked chicklit. You only have to look at the Gertie McDowell segment in *Ulysses*. In fact he submitted some of his early efforts to Mills & Boon.

Declan Kiberd

While I was at UCD I edited a literary magazine. I wrote a lot of the stories under pseudonyms because we didn't have enough people to fill it. I would make up biographies for these pseudonyms: 'Seamus MacChommaraigh was born in the Donegal Gaeltacht in 1953 and is at present serving in a ministerial capacity in Ghana.'

Gabriel Byrne

Nothing brings a writer back to reality quicker than arriving at a bookshop in a rainy Northern English town on a book tour only to find the pallid and overworked staff trying to spread out and look like a crowd.

Joe O'Connor

The key word in my plays is 'Perhaps'.

Samuel Beckett

I want a poem I can grow old in. I want a poem I can die in.

Eavan Boland

Writers are a scourge to those they cohabit with.

Edna O'Brien

Writing is a curious business. The true believer can find more excitement in creating a one-liner or a metaphor or even a pun than in getting a message from Meryl Streep that she wishes to share the rest of her life with him.

Con Houlihan

A journalist should always be an outsider.

Douglas Gageby

Poetry is language in orbit.

Seamus Heaney

I'll write until I die.

Nell McCafferty

I come from a long line of unpublishable Tiernans who have novels in the closet.

Tommy Tiernan

My entire involvement with the Irish Literary Revival consisted of standing beside W.B. Yeats in the urinal during an interval at the Abbey Theatre, where I remember he was having great difficulty with his waterworks.

Eoin O'Mahony

I started with Heaney. You started to cough.

Rita Ann Higgins

Poetry is bad enough without it being long as well.

John B. Keane

Characters aren't created by writers. They pre-exist and have to be found.

Elizabeth Bowen

The modern generation seems to have forgotten the art of page-turning. Did you hear about the little girl who received a book from her Daddy one Christmas morning and didn't know what to do with it because there was no place to put the batteries?

Brian Behan

How is it they always overlook Anon when they're giving out literary awards?

John B. Keane

The great enemy of art is the ego.

Paul Durcan

To be a published poet is not a sane person's aspiration.

Bernard O'Donoghue

Have you ever seen a statue erected to a critic?

Daniel O'Donnell

If I couldn't write I'd go stone fucking mad.

John B. Keane

I never spoke to John Banville without feeling like the janitor's son approaching the headmaster at a public school.

Fergal Keane

I think of my novels as sonnet sequences.

John Banville

All her life to labour, and labour for Faber and Faber.

Seamus Heaney

Sometimes when things are going really well I back away from the desk and wander around and fill the fridge, or I go down to the shops for a bottle of milk that I don't need.

Roddy Doyle

Dublin critics know everything about everything. You can't stand for five minutes sheltering from the rain without being told you just made a bollocks of it.

Lee Dunne

A writer's opinion on anything is no more interesting than a footballer's.

John McGahern

'What can we give our local TD for his birthday?'
'A book.'
'Ah no. He's got one of them already.'

Myler McGrath

Writers of fiction are collectors of useless information.

William Trevor

I started writing plays because I felt I wasn't going to be able to. If you can, why bother?

Tom Murphy

Hamlet is a terrific play but there are too many quotations in it.

Hugh Leonard

The writer's greatest asset is his indignation.

John B. Keane

Waiting for Godot is a play in which nothing happens twice.

Hugh Kenner

I'm writing an Irish trilogy. It has four books in it.

Brendan O'Carroll

If a writer says he doesn't read reviews of his work, his nose will grow longer and longer until eventually it falls off.

Hugh Leonard

A man will give up on a book as rubbish if a character doesn't get killed, have sex with a stranger or show signs of having a Nazi past within the first twenty pages. Women, on the other hand, will stick with the chick-lit tale of Angie, a twenty-something career girl who loves Chardonnay and saucy flings with divine stockbrokers, but longs to marry an older doctor. If Angie dies with a swastika on her knickers, you could also nail the male market.

Pat Fitzpatrick

Acid Drops

Garage flowers should only be purchased when going to visit someone in a coma, and even then you'd better pray that they don't wake up.

Graham Norton

All modern architects should be pulled down and redeveloped as car parks.

Spike Milligan

Colin Montgomerie couldn't count his balls and get the same answer twice.

David Feherty

The only thing I ever had in common with Ernest Blythe was that I could tell him to fuck off in Irish.

Brendan Behan

I'm looking forward to being really old so that I can lean over in a restaurant and say to my son: 'I just pissed myself. Deal with it.'

Dylan Moran

The biggest obstruction on the M50 is the toll booth.

Shane Ross

Most human beings are quite likeable if you don't see too much of them.

Robert Lynd

I hope this isn't an isolated incident.

Ian Paisley after the murder of three IRA members in Gibraltar in 1988

Bono is a little shit.

Gerry Adams in 1983

Lawyers are people who prove that talk definitely isn't cheap.

Justine McCarthy

He's completely unspoiled by failure.

Frank Carson

In Ireland we have nine to ten months of bad weather. Then winter sets in.

David Feherty

I won't say it was the worst match I ever saw, but I'm going to tape the weather report over it.

Gene Fitzpatrick

Michael Flatley reminds me of someone with a spud stuck up his arse who's trying to squeeze it out without using his hands.

David Feherty

What do I think of agents? Dogs, worms, vermin.

Joe Kinnear

My uncle was an angry man. He had printed on his grave: 'What are you lookin' at?'

Margaret Smith

Humans are the only species that systematically tortures and murders its own for pleasure and personal gain. All our poems and symphonies and oils on canvas will never change that.

George Carlin

If I've ever offended anyone in any of my acts I'd like to say, from the bottom of my heart…I couldn't give a fuck.

Brendan O'Carroll

I'm not sure when exactly I rejoined the 'real' world after my heart surgery. I do remember, however, the nurses insisting that I must walk. 'Put your head and shoulder back,' instructed the nurse. 'Come on, lift your feet.' 'But I can't lift my foot,' I protested. 'You must walk,' insisted the nurse. 'Were you in Stalag 17?' I asked.

Jimmy Magee

A man said to me, 'Come here, Shit-For-Brains'. I said, 'Is that an offer of a swap?'

Michael Mee

I was appearing in Washington once and they told me they had a 'language policy' so I couldn't swear. I thought to myself: 'What the fuck!'

Tommy Tiernan

When I discovered I had no aptitude for any job I joined the civil service.

Moss Keane

Cilla Black has quit *Blind Date* after 18 years. She says the show finally became more work than fun. Now you know what it's like to watch it, Cilla.

Patrick Kielty

Cannabis has been changed from a Class B drug to Class C, which was a nightmare for Scouse kids. They had to learn a new letter.

Jimmy Carr

When is a celebrity not a celebrity? When you'd pass them by in the supermarket in a rush to buy the Cat-lit without secretly congratulating yourself on being cool enough not to have looked like you noticed them – because you didn't.

Hilary Fannin

Out of every 14 people who watch *Coronation Street*, 12 of them are morons.

Sean Hughes

No more hanging. What's this country coming to?

Patrick McCabe

If Sinéad O'Connor was singing for her supper she'd sleep out as far as I was concerned.

Paddy Cole

Rugby people. Can't live with them, can't shoot them.

Tom Humphries

Every time I give someone a leading part I make one friend and ten enemies.

Michael Colgan

The *Irish Press* dipped in circulation for a complexity of reasons. One was the fact that it catered for people who couldn't buy it because they were dead.

Con Houlihan

Brian Friel always listened avidly to your suggestions. And then he always rejected them.

Vincent Dowling

The secret of doing the waltz perfectly is to behave as if your partner has BO.

Gloria Hunniford

Naomi Campbell takes enough transatlantic flights to have a hole in the ozone named after her.

Aingeala Flannery

A friend of mine went to the doctor because he was getting chest pains. The doctor told him he needed to reduce the stress points in his life. My friend asked, 'How do I do that?' The doctor replied, 'Avoid excitement. Watch the Dubs.'

Pat Spillane

I wouldn't thank you at all for giving me the most wonderful part in a pile of shit.

Donal McCann

I'd like to congratulate Belvedere College on the great job they did in teaching Tony O'Reilly to speak so well. It's just a pity they didn't teach him how to stop.

Bertie Ahern

When a priest warned my father to get into the church fast or face an eternity roaring in the flames, he responded with a remark that would earn him the status of local legend. 'My good man,' he said, 'your fulminations have the same effect on me as the fart of a blackbird on the water levels of the Grand Coolee dam.'

Fergal Keane

I suppose that's the knighthood fucked.

George Best after being arrested for drunk driving

The new Irish Dream is the American Dream with bad weather.

David McWilliams

I hear there's someone dead belonging to you. It wouldn't be yourself by any chance, would it?

Brendan Behan

Have you ever wondered why you never see a High Court judge out and about? There's a very simple reason. They don't live on this planet.

Pat Flanagan

If you aren't depressed going into St Brendan's in Grangegorman, you will be coming out of it.

Donal Ruane

Eamon Dunphy has the unique ability to irritate the teats off a cow.

Pat Stacey

'Veteran' is a euphemism for 'decrepit'.

Terry Wogan

Carla Bruni is so flat-chested she could iron her top with it on.

Barry Egan

Bono once said to me, 'Why the fuck are you still a priest?'

Fr Brian D'Arcy

The Irish language is guttural. I trained myself to speak it by watching Al Jazeera television broadcasts.

Des Bishop

Her vocabulary would strip paint from a hall door.

Hugh Leonard

Most of the people who ran RTE in the old days thought it was a lovely place – apart from those troublesome oafs who presented the programmes.

Gay Byrne

Italy had more misses than Henry VIII.

Bill O'Herlihy

If I had it all over again I would never darken the door of a theatre. I can't stand this stupid business.

Twink

There's something wonderfully erotic about a stunningly beautiful woman effing and blinding.

Paul Byrne

For 90 minutes a week Paul McGrath was the bravest footballer in Britain, but for the other 166½ hours he was a child.

Jim Walker

My magic words at half-time were fuck, balls, bollox, crap and piss-poor.

Mick McCarthy

The nurse shoved a rectal thermometer at me but I told her what she could do with it.

Shaun Connors

Is that my friend in the bunker or is the bastard on the green?

David Feherty

The main problem with *Riverdance* is that it makes Irish dancers look happy, which was never the way in my time.

Maureen Potter

Wedded Blitz

Marriage is the main cause of divorce.

Richard Harris

I would never have married a man like Charlie Haughey. As a mistress you see the best side of someone. They're dressed up, going somewhere nice to meet you, and anticipating having a bit of fun. You're not talking about school reports or the bathroom leaking.

Terry Keane

Marriage begins when you sink in his arms, and ends with your arms in his sink.

Maureen Potter

Niagara Falls is the second biggest disappointment of the average honeymoon.

Oscar Wilde

I knew a man who was so industrious he went on his honeymoon alone, leaving his wife at home to mind the shop.

Jack Cruise

When I got divorced I went through the various stages of grieving: anger, denial, dancing round my settlement cheque...

Maura Kennedy

I cannot stand the shows so often put on by married people to insinuate that they are not only more fortunate but in some way more moral than you are.

Iris Murdoch

When you're young you think of marriage as a train you simply have to catch. You run and run until you've caught it, and then you sit back and look out the window and realise you're bored.

Elizabeth Bowen

I said to my girlfriend's father, 'I'd like to marry your daughter.' He said, 'Have you seen her mother?' 'I have,' I told him, 'but I still want to marry your daughter.'

Shaun Connors

You want to know the difference between my wife and a terrorist? You can negotiate with a terrorist.

Frank Carson

I'd like to get married again but I'm afraid of the commitment. I mean we're talking two, even three years of my life here.

Maura Kennedy

The older you get, the more you lower your standards. I used to be so picky. 'Oh, when I get married he's going to be tall, handsome, rich.' Now I'm down to 'Registered voter'.

Kathleen Madigan

There's no stigma today to what was once called 'living in sin', a locution that has to be explained to a younger generation, who greet it with incredulous hilarity.

Mary Kenny

I've never regretted a moment of life with my wife. She's beautiful. She's gorgeous. She's listening.

Brendan O'Carroll

I once received 100 marriage proposals in a three-week period.

Eileen Reid

Statistics show that the older you are when you get married, the more likely it is you'll stay together. Of course, because at 85 you can't hear how boring he is.

Christine O'Rourke

Janet Reno inserted an advert in the classifieds: 'Husband wanted'. The next day she received 100 letters. They all said the same thing: 'You can have mine'.

John Scally

My wife just told me the good news: I'm going to be a dad for the first time. The bad news is that we already have two kids.

Brian Kiely

They say moving house and divorce are the most traumatic events in a person's life. Well I've tried both and I'd take the courts every time.

Róisín Ingle

I once went to a furniture shop with my wife to buy a coffee table. We couldn't find one we both liked so we compromised and bought one we both hated.

Michael Redmond

On the subject of gay marriage, one wag said he believed in it because he felt gays should suffer as much as the rest of us.

Mary Kenny

There's a curious statistic I came across recently. The average married couple converse for twenty minutes every week. What do they find to talk about?

Dave Allen

I'd marry a midget just for the handicapped parking.

Kathleen Madigan

I arranged my wedding day for 29 December, which meant that the previous six month's hard-won weight loss was annihilated in a matter of minutes on Christmas Eve when I interfaced with a wheelie-bin size of Roses.

Marian Keyes

Gay marriage will never work. It's difficult enough when you have even *one* man in a marriage.

Graham Norton

I don't think my wife likes me very much. When I had a heart attack she *wrote* for an ambulance.

Frank Carson

I know a woman who had her husband cremated and then mixed his ashes with grass and smoked him. She said it was the best he'd made her feel for years.

Maureen Murphy

I met my wife when her television company wanted to option one of my books. She couldn't afford the book so she got me instead.

Joe O'Connor

In modern families the children don't live at home until after they're married.

Rosaleen Linehan

How can you tell if your wife is dead? The sex is the same but the dishes are higher in the sink.

Brendan Grace

Loving your wife isn't enough. You also have to like her.

Dickie Rock

George Bush reminds every woman of her first husband.

Jane O'Reilly

I knew an eighty-five-year-old man who married a girl of eighteen. He wanted someone to answer the Rosary for him.

Éamon Kelly

A man said to his friend, 'My wife is an angel.'
The friend replied, 'You're lucky, mine is still alive.'

Shaun Connors

After a few years of marriage your get up and go has got up and gone.

Conal Gallen

Having separated parents is my idea of normal.

Cecelia Ahern

GOLF TIPS

I love golf so much I played last week instead of attending a wedding. My own.

Joe O'Donovan

Never ever drink and drive. It impairs judgment, and makes it harder to get power into your backswing.

David Kenny

Spain's Guadiana course has more out of bounds than Alcatraz.

Christy O'Connor Jr

I play with fear. Fear isn't a good thing to play with, but it's successful. I've never had much success with confidence.

Pádraig Harrington

I usually play 18 holes with a friend of mine who's a priest. Last Sunday he couldn't make up his mind whether to go to church or to the golf course so he tossed a coin. The reason he was late was because he had to toss it seventeen times.

Dave O'Gorman

Bumpy greens don't bother me any more. Since I've become an analyst I don't see the problem.

David Feherty

Good news: ten golfers a year are hit by lightning.

George Carlin

The Darren Clarke Syndrome may be described as an inexplicable affection for dodgy trousers.

Bill Elliott

I can never understand the male obsession with golf. How can guys be so enamoured of a game where they try to get a relatively large ball into a relatively small hole when the same lads find it next to impossible to get a thin stream of urine into the gaping chasm of the toilet.

Anne Marie Scanlon

I hit a shot into the trees once when I was suffering from a hangover but there was method in my madness. I had a man in there with a flask of coffee and a hair of the dog.

Christy O'Connor

I thought I'd encountered every hazard, but on this course you have to take into account the curvature of the earth.

David Feherty on the Crooked Stick course during the 1991 PGA Championship

Asking Jack Nicklaus to redesign Augusta was like asking Andy Warhol to repaint the Sistine Chapel.

David Feherty

I wouldn't know a nine-iron from a steam iron.

Lise Hand

Playing golf is like having a second passport – into people's lives.

Joe Carr

Golf is the easiest game of all to play badly.

Kevin Flanagan

There are now more golf courses in Ireland than children's playgrounds.

David McWilliams

Golf is a game in which you wet yourself laughing at your best friend's misfortune. He won't hold it against you because he knows your turn is coming.

David Feherty

The fervent hordes progress with unshakeable faith from the altar of the first tee to the shrine of the green. Yea, though they walk through the valley of the squelching muck, they feel no distress: for Tiger is with them.

Miriam Lord

Bringing Ireland's first Ryder Cup to the charmless Palmer course is like having Keira Knightley invite you to her bedroom to move furniture. It's like going to Rome for dinner and ordering fish and chips.

Bruce Selcraig on Ireland's hosting of the 2006 Ryder Cup in the K Club

I'm the big brash fella who gives the ball a massive wallop and doesn't give a fiddler's toss where it ends up.

Ronan Rafferty

When the wind blows on the course in Rosses Point, the only hiding place is the clubhouse.

Cecil Ewing

My caddy found my ball in the bushes after an hour. I told him it looked very old. 'It's a long time since we started, sir,' he replied.

Frank Carson

Crass corporate elitism meets native genius for price gouging and pat insecurity.

Tom Humphries on the Ryder Cup

When you play from a rough lie your buttocks are clamped as you pray that the recipient of the venomous swipe doesn't fly out like a wounded snipe across the green into the same crap.

David Feherty

There's no such thing as a lovely swing. You hit it like an axe murderer? Fair play. Hit it.

Tom Humphries

Des Cahill stealthily creeping across the grass as he wheezed quietly into the microphone sounded like an emphysemic David Attenborough trying to get close to a family of gorillas.

Miriam Lord

The way Colin Montgomerie stands, he looks like he's just done something in his pants. Or, worse still, is actually in the process of doing it.

Fergus Shanley

If I were asked to rewrite the rules of golf I'd add just one new one: 'Players may be allowed to tackle their opponents.'

David Feherty

My golf partner told me I was the most consistent player he knew. 'Some hole in one putt,' he said, 'and some in two, but you never fail to hole in three.'

John B. Keane

Early yesterday morning Sky TV informed us that Colin Montgomerie played hockey in his youth. Two words: 'Mind' and 'boggles'.

Mary Hannigan

The Ryder Cup is little more than an expensive pandering to the bloated egos of a small group of cosseted millionaires.

Lise Hand

Being seven shots behind gives you a definite psychological advantage.

Alex Murphy

I was so tense I could hear the bees farting.

Mick O'Loughlin

Second sucks.

Pádraig Harrington

The Fatkins Diet

If they don't have chocolate in heaven, I'm not going.

June Rodgers

Even when I was at my thinnest, there was always a fat woman inside me waiting to get out.

Marian Keyes

I don't think we should use words like obese, big-boned or overweight when we mean fat. Obese is a medical term. Dinosaurs are big-boned but not overweight. Overweight implies that there is some correct weight. Heavy is also a misleading term. An aircraft carrier is heavy; it's not fat. Only people are fat and that's what fat people are. They're fat.

George Carlin

The man ahead of me in the Starbucks queue the other day ordered something called 'A tall skinny latte with an extra shot'. Of course they knew exactly what he meant. When it came to my turn I held my nerve and asked for a small black coffee. I'm a Starbucksspeak refusenik.

Frank McNally

He's put on weight and I've lost it, and vice versa.

Ronnie Whelan

On my first day in RTE, when mealtime came, I went to the canteen for lunch. 'What are my choices?' I asked. The man behind the counter replied, 'Yes or no'.

Pat Spillane

Faith can move mountains…she's a pretty big girl.

Graffiti

If you currently look like a Sumo wrestler, don't expect to look like Elle McPherson after a couple of goes on the Stairmaster.

Anne Marie Scanlon

'What are you giving up for Lent?' my father said. 'Grapes,' I replied. 'We never have grapes,' he said.

Bob Geldof

People say your belly button has no function but it's an ideal place to put the salt if you're having a Big Mac in the scratcher.

Shay O'Donoghue

I love the way the Irish language puts things. 'Tá ocras orm'. Hunger is on me. Like a backpack.

Des Bishop

I was so fat when I was young I thought I stood a better chance of being a comedy actor, like John Candy, than a singer.

Bryan McFadden

I can cook a mean salmon and pasta risotto but don't ask me to try to boil an egg correctly or make toast without burning it.

Siobhán Cronin

I'm quite convinced that in about ten or twenty years time when you buy food it will have a message on it saying: 'Warning: Food is Dangerous to Your Health'.

Dave Allen

I'm a presenter, not a model. I have curves. I like my dinner.

Gráinne Seoige

Coffee is a language unto itself. If someone asked you for a tall skinny sleeper with whip, would you return with a six foot three, underweight Al Qaeda operative with an S&M fetish instead of a decaf latte with two shots of espresso, low-fat milk and whipped cream?

Paul Howard

I've never cooked a meal in my life and never intend to. In a list of activities that are a complete waste of valuable time during our short stay on this earth, cooking jostles for the number one spot with gardening, polishing shoes and cleaning Venetian blinds.

Donal Ruane

There's a big boom in Irish culture right now. I was in Barnes & Noble the other day and I saw a book entitled *Irish Cuisine* and I almost laughed my balls off. What are we famous for, cuisine-wise? We put everything in a pot and we boil it for seventeen-and-a-half hours straight, until you can eat it with a straw. That's not cuisine, that's penance.

Denis Leary

I make a lot of jokes about vegetarians in my act but most of them don't have the strength to protest.

Ardal O'Hanlon

The only reason I've been called the strong silent type is because I find it difficult to talk to women when I'm trying to hold my stomach in.

Pat Ingoldsby

I eat to keep my mind off food.

Brendan Grace

Just how skinny is Victoria Beckham? If you hugged her, would she break? We know that she wears jeans with a twenty-three-inch waist – the size, apparently, of a seven-year-old child. It also happens to be the circumference of my head.

Sophie Haslett

The only exercise I get these days is coughing.

Alex Higgins

Pamela Anderson is the ideal beach cop lifeguard. If there's a problem at sea she just lies on her back and turns into a life raft.

Pat Shortt

My colleagues and I have shared a curry at 8.15 in the morning and been the better for it. People think you can't eat and broadcast at the same time. Pshaw!

Terry Wogan

It seems the only way to have a healthy life nowadays is not to eat. Starve to death. At least when you're dying you'll know it isn't of anything serious.

Dave Allen

I've never followed a diet, never bought a diet book, never counted a calorie. Life's too short. I could go to sleep on a bed of mashed potato.

Graham Norton

My doctor told me to exercise. He said walking would get me into shape. 'I already have a shape,' I told him. 'It's round'.

Brendan Grace

I could eat a baby's arse through the bars of a cot.

Dara O'Briain

I owe my six-pack to my constant state of nervous tension, which causes me to literally burn off all the calories, even when I'm just sitting there. I'm constantly being exhorted by my colleagues to eat more. I urge them to calm themselves. 'I eat every bit as much as you,' I explain, 'but the weight just won't stay on.'

Terry Wogan

I don't own a computer. I'm waiting for the kind where I can look in the screen and say, 'Hey, I need a pizza' and one comes out and hits me in the eyebrows.

Kathleen Madigan

I'm on a sea-food diet. Whenever I see food I eat it.

Derek Davis

People like Carol Vorderman have the arrogance to think I want a body like theirs. What I want is a body like mine. But could I have it in a smaller size, please?

Róisín Ingle

If someone says they're on a diet I think it's perfectly fair if they tell you quietly, but it's destructive and anti-celebratory if they say it like a Christian martyr during the meal and make everyone else feel guilty and gluttonous.

Maeve Binchy

I was briefly a restaurant critic. If ever there was someone who should not be a restaurant critic, that person is me. Like most people, I like food but I do not consider it to be a religious experience.

Deirdre Purcell

There's no such thing as gourmet coffee, gourmet rolls or gourmet pizza. Gourmet means one thing: 'We're going to charge you more.'

George Carlin

Stories about the glamorous lifestyles of strict fitness regimes of celebs leave me cold. I much prefer to read about them sacking the stylist, buying stretch waistbands, or diving face-first into a vat of ice-cream.

Martina Devlin

It's a statistical fact that a pizza will reach your house faster than an ambulance. So the next time you've taken a bad turn, speed-dial the local fast food joint instead of 999.

June Rodgers

The only problem with the restaurant in the National Gallery is that you have to go through the gallery to get to it.

Paul Durcan

Images of Lindsay Lohan's chest bones reaching out to greet strangers, or Keira Knightley's xylophone of vertebrae, countable at thirty paces, have burned themselves into our consciousness so that über-thin no longer looks odd.

Sophie Haslett

The Last Supper in the *Titanic* dining room was a lavish affair, consisting of something in the order of twelve courses. No wonder it sank so quickly.

Dan Buckley

My idea of perfection is a man who turns into a pizza after sex.

Deirdre Walsh

There's nothing worse than being stuck up in the Andes after a plane crash with your anorexic buddy.

Denis Leary

Irish coffee is the only drink that provides all four essentials: alcohol, caffeine, sugar and fat.

Danny McGrath

No matter what you ask for in an American restaurant, they'll say 'Do you want cheese with that?' One day I lost my temper. 'I asked for a fucking newspaper!' I said.

Tommy Tiernan

Self-Abuse

Before becoming an actor I had a brief but disastrous flirtation with journalism. I was offered a book to review, read it twice, thought about it for three weeks, and then found I had nothing to say.

Daniel Day-Lewis

I was on the dole for six years and then they started to train me. After that I finally knew what kind of work I was out of.

Conal Gallen

Every Wednesday I get my free copy of the *RTE Guide*. The first thing I do is open the radio pages to see if I'm on next week.

Joe Duffy

I can happily stand on my head when asked, but when it comes to balancing awkwardly in an upright position I stagger around like Long John Silver on LSD.

Siobhán Cronin

I'd love to blow my own trumpet but the work's too hard.

Sean O'Casey

I'd be a goner now if I did everything I wrote.

Edna O'Brien

I'm just a voyeur who lives off other people's tragedies.

Anthony Clare

I'm a pacifist by physique.

Michael Mee

I'm a product slut. If face creams were husbands, then I'm Elizabeth Taylor.

Marian Keyes

I've been working on accepting my inner scumbag.

George Carlin

I'm not quick. If I go out running, women with prams pass me out.

Mick McCarthy

I was kept back in High Infants so long, my teacher wanted to adopt me.

James McKeon

I have two very expensive vices. I smoke cigars and live in Ireland.

Ronnie Drew

Some days I could thread the ball through the eye of a needle. On others I couldn't put it into a bucket.

Christy O'Connor

I started my life with nothing, had plenty in the middle, and ended with nothing again. That's the cycle.

Joe Carr

I have an ideal face for radio.

Ryan Tubridy

I'm attracted to tall, thin, good-looking men who have one thing in common: they must be lurking bastards.

Edna O'Brien

Last night I was lying in bed with the wife. I was lying to her and she was lying to me.

Brendan Grace

I never finish anything I st

Graffiti

One of the enjoyable things about journalism is that you can write something on a Friday and see it in print on a Saturday. The fact that it's in the bin by Sunday doesn't really matter.

Joe O'Connor

I spent five years in hospital before I was 20, which marks a child. You're completely alone. You're not experimenting with the boys and the lipstick and all that stuff. I became a serious, boring sod.

Brenda Fricker

I'm so small, my first job was a lumberjack in a mushroom factory. I later went on to become a podiatrist for Dolly Parton but quit because I don't like working in the dark.

Noel V. Ginnity

I left *Morning Call* because I ran out of clichés.

Mike Murphy

I now have the level of fame where people either think they know me from the telly or from putting out the bins four doors up.

Sean Hughes

I left teaching because I didn't want to be still there at seventy in white hair and a stained waistcoat and the kids saying, 'Oh no, not this eejit again.'

Gabriel Byrne

The first autograph I was asked to sign was on a girl's arm. I couldn't believe it. Me, a guy from Cabra West.

Dickie Rock

I was without doubt the worst library assistant ever to work for the Dublin County Council. Perhaps there was some previous claimant to this title, but if so they must have bricked him up alive in a cavity in a wall behind the non-fiction section in some remote branch library.

Dermot Bolger

My wife often remarks that it's a good job I can laugh at myself, because I have so many reasons to.

Pat Spillane

I was a nerd in university, spending my time either at lectures, tutorials or studying in the library. How sad is that?

Mary Kennedy

I can't cook. I can't fix things. I'm technologically illiterate. I can't put up a shelf.

Michael Colgan

I'm not very wild. I tried to trash hotel rooms when I was younger but I always ended up making the bed – and leaving a small chocolate on the pillow for the maid.

Ardal O'Hanlon

Some of my best work has been fuelled by the fear that it might turn out to be my worst.

Róisín Ingle

I don't have a good self-image. When I go to rugby matches I suspect the players are gossiping about me in the scrums.

Liam Kennedy

I was born with a tongue-tie, a restrictive piece of skin under the tongue. The doctor snipped it with a special pair of silver scissors. My mom later said, 'I sometimes wonder if we did the right thing!'

Gloria Hunniford

I used to go to an analyst who made me blame all my problems on my mother. I now have a new one. He tells me it's all my fault. It's a kind of relief.

Tom Walsh

I'm dyslexic. There was a sign outside my school that said, 'Slow Children'. Which didn't do much for my self-esteem. Then again, I couldn't read it.

Jimmy Carr

I sing only to punish my children.

David Feherty

I was ordained at the age of 24. 24 going on 11.

Fr Brian D'Arcy

I'm so short I'm the only person in the world whose feet are in his passport photograph.

Noel V. Ginnity

I only scored one rugby try in my life. It happened because I slipped on the ball as it was going over the line.

Charlie Bird

What do I know of man's destiny? I could tell you more about radishes.

Samuel Beckett

If I could afford a nervous breakdown I'd give it away to someone more deserving.

John B. Keane

I love arguments. If you tell me the sky is royal blue I'll say, 'No, that's azure blue.' I'd argue that with you for ten minutes. Then the next guy will come long and tell me the sky is azure blue and I'll say, 'No, no, that's royal blue.'

Pádraig Harrington

Don't ever put yourself up for auction. It can be a shock to discover how little you're worth.

Olivia O'Leary

I'm so pessimistic I'm even pessimistic about the pessimism of other pessimists.

Ed Byrne

I can't swim. I can't drive either. I was going to learn to drive but then I thought: What if I crash into a lake?

Dylan Moran

I only started liking Jennifer Aniston after Brad Pitt dumped her. I'm riveted by Renée Zellweger's failure to keep a man. And I grow fonder of Cameron Diaz every time she's photographed with yet another skin eruption.

Martina Devlin

I'm glad I'm not bisexual. I couldn't stand being rejected by men as well as women.

Joe Dennehy

My handwriting is so bad I can't even read it myself.

Roddy Doyle

When I look at one of my paintings, all I see are the mistakes.

Graham Knuttel

I have a terrible memory for names. I wish everyone in the world wore invisible name tags and I was the only one who could see them, so I could flick over them with my eyes and remember the names of their children and all about their sister's operation.

Michael Colgan

I've spent more time in my life dreaming than thinking. In many ways I missed it. It passed me by while I wasn't paying attention.

Richard Harris

I'm on so many pills that when I drop dead my coffin will have a child-proof lid.

Paul O'Grady

At the beginning of my golfing career I could have built a whole new golf course from my divots.

Joe Carr

I swing like a toilet door on a prawn trawler.

David Feherty

I gave up trying to be God in 1970.

Fr Brian D'Arcy

We forged our own music because we couldn't play other people's very well.

Bono

People have accused me of being so far up Tiger Woods's arse he can barely make a full swing,

David Feherty

I've looked 76 for 40 years.

David Kelly

I failed all my exams at school so I could go to art school.

Graham Knuttel

With a nose as big as mine, cocaine would be a very expensive habit.

Chris de Burgh

My critics have told me I've ruined the lives of 50 million people. I can't be certain of this since only about ten million have actually come back to thank me.

Denis Leary

I gave up hurling when one of my teachers told me to cut five inches off my hurley. I asked him if it was too big for me, and he said, 'No, but it will fit into the bin more easily like that.'

Pat Spillane

The last time we played Seville we were beaten 2–0. And we were lucky to get nil.

Mick McCarthy

I still don't know what I'll be when I grow up.

Vincent Dowling

I came out of the education system as a dedicated, bright, lazy Leaving-Certer with five honours. And I knew nothing.

Gabriel Fitzmaurice

I never had illusions about being a beauty – I was the only seventeen-year-old character actress in movies.

Angela Lansbury

I look like a depressed hyena.

David Kelly

Many years ago I decided to kill myself by jumping off Dún Laoghaire pier because I felt fat, balding, toothless and useless.

George Hook

I write equally badly with both hands.

Vincent Dowling

I had a colleague years ago who used to smile and say that she was always late as if it was something outside her control, like having freckles or a Gemini star sign.

Maeve Binchy

I love to smoke so much I'm going to have a tracheotomy so I can have two at the same time.

Denis Leary

All my bits are wearing out. I hear funny little clicking sounds in my knees when I walk. My left arm has almost given up the ghost. The only place on my entire body where I still have black hair is inside my nostrils.

Pat Ingoldsby

I'm a terrible lover. The best I can give a woman is an anticlimax.

Des Sheehy

I got my figure back after giving birth. It's a pity I didn't get someone else's!

Aisling Haverty

At school I prayed I *wouldn't* get a vocation for the priesthood.

Terry Wogan

He was also terrified of me, because I had switched into bubbly/amusing mode and he thought I was like that all the time and how would he work with me without braining me for this babble?

Terry Prone on meeting Howard Kinley

Animal Farm

Cats have nine lives, which makes them ideal for experimentation.
Jimmy Carr

After I was bitten by an adder at the PGA Championships I considered beating the living daylights out of it. But then I thought: it's probably got a wife and snakelets to look after.
David Feherty

The reason there are no dogs on the moon is because there are no trees up there.
Dave Allen

Why aren't the Mayo team allowed to own a dog? Because they can't hold on to a lead.
Tom O'Hora

Why is it that when the doorbell rings the dog always thinks it's for him?
Noel V. Ginnity

I'm the only boxer in my family. All the rest of us were Alsatians.
Barry McGuigan

My dog can read. When he saw a sign saying 'Wet Paint', he did.

Shaun Connors

I'm very, very afraid of dogs, even nice dogs. Most dog-owners simply insist I just haven't met the right dog yet.

Marian Keyes

One of Heather Mills's many claims to mediocrity is the fact that, unlike the rest of us plebeian scum, she likes animals.

Ian O'Doherty

I hope they clone dinosaurs and they come back just in time for the ozone layer to disappear so we can wipe those ugly motherfuckers out again.

George Carlin

Do you know what they say when they geld a race horse? 'And they're off!'

Conan O'Brien

How would you know if your goldfish was incontinent?

Ray Fitzgerald

Who knows what the ostrich sees in the sand?

Samuel Beckett

I once taught English to Spanish soldiers. I had to say things like 'Rex has the ball. "Woof, woof," says Rex.' I remember saying, 'What does Rex say?' and fifty big macho soldiers in crewcuts would say back, 'Woof woof.'

Gabriel Byrne

I've been thinking of marrying a horse. We'd have a stable relationship.

Shane Filan

In politics I much prefer the Rottweiler to the poodle. He gets more done.

Mary Harney

The highlight of our stay in Cayenne, French Guiana, was the time we saw a dog crossing the street. We still talk about it.

Hector Ó hEochagáin

A Kerry schoolmaster used to say that from walking behind their bullocks the Roscommon men and women have become like them.

John McGahern

Just as a cat will leap on the lap of the one person in the room who hates animals, I have always and disastrously been a magnet for my natural enemies.

Hugh Leonard

I started a PhD in English at the University of Chicago because I loved poetry, which I now realise is like saying I studied vivisection because I loved dogs.

Michael Donaghy

I don't understand evolution. If we came from monkeys why are there still monkeys?

Kathleen Madigan

I met a farmer one day outside Dungarvan. We were making conversation about his cattle. 'You have a few horses too,' I said as I heard the clip of hooves down the lane. 'Ah, you'd have to,' he said, 'There's no romance in cows.'

Olivia O'Leary

Sport is a serious business. You prepare very hard. You sacrifice an awful lot, but when you go home your dog will still greet you, irrespective of the result.

Sean Boylan

Any tiger, if it's pursued too much, will turn, and I would imagine the Celtic tiger will turn and whoever is closest at the time will get hurt.

Daniel O'Donnell

My house is like Animal Rescue on A&E night with four cats, three dogs, a gecko, a red-kneed tarantula named Chevy and several tanks of psychotic fish.

Kate Holmquist

My granny wore a hearing aid that she kept at low because whenever she turned it up it whistled, and every dog in Dublin rushed to her side.

Terry Wogan

They've now approved a Prozac-type drug for dogs who are depressed. This is good because it's hard for dogs to get therapy since they're never allowed on the couch.

Colin Quinn

I was born on my sister's fourth birthday. I wasn't exactly the present she had in mind. Apparently she took one look at my scrawny red face and howled, 'But I wanted a puppy!'

Gloria Hunniford

Sometimes I get more excited about a horse winning a race than I do over a performance I've given.

Donal McCann

Two things are traditionally killed off at Christmas: turkeys and soap characters.

Chris Barry

Why should I exercise? The longest-living animal is the tortoise.

Terry Wogan

The best way to smuggle drugs these days is to stuff them up a dog's arse. The airport officials will think the sniffer dogs are just getting frisky.

Ardal O'Hanlon

Sheep are evil. They've got no eyebrows. You never know if what you're saying to them has any effect.

Tommy Tiernan

Sign in a vet's office: 'Back In Ten Minutes. Sit!'

Joe McNamara

Don't kick the dog to see if it's still sleeping.

Gerry Adams

One of my pupils once described a zebra as 'A horse with Venetian blinds'.

Bryan MacMahon

A man walks into a butcher shop. 'Have you got a sheep's head?' he asks. 'No,' the butcher replies, 'It's the way I comb my hair'.

Shaun Connors

Liam is gone to the zoo. The monkeys are bringing their kids to look at him.

Noel Gallagher on his brother

Cats only jump into your lap to find out if you're cold enough to eat.

Anne Enright

If I fry you an egg, at the end of the enterprise the kitchen is going to look like a deranged bison has been doing salsa dancing on every surface.

Terry Prone

The Rag Trade

I wanted fame so badly I would have run across a football pitch naked.

Samantha Mumba

The definition of a yuppie is a man who has different gardening clothes for his front and back garden.

Des McCarthy

There we were in the middle of a sexual revolution, wearing clothes that guaranteed we wouldn't get laid.

Denis Leary on the 1960s

I don't spend a fortune on clothes. Not with a face like I have.

Roy Keane

My mother only commented on my clothes once. She said, 'Nell, will you get a frock for my funeral?'

Nell McCafferty

That's a beautiful dress you're almost wearing.

Stephen Boyd to Brigitte Bardot on the set of *Shalako*

I did most of the interviews for *Morning Ireland* in my underwear.

Liz O'Donnell

If there's a single common complaint from all of the children I get as a house-husband, it's to do with finding the wrong knickers in their drawers, if you follow me.

Kevin Murphy

Last night my girlfriend was wearing a dress so tight I could hardly breathe.

Sean Kilroy

My mother was seven hours in labour. They forgot to take her tights off.

James McKeon

I like unclothed bodies, but only when they're female and nubile. The male of the species isn't nude, but naked.

Hugh Leonard

Her T-shirt said, 'Mongoloid Porn Inferno'. All I could think was: That sounds like a busy evening.

Dylan Moran

In my mother's day if you set foot outside the door with a matching handbag and shoes you were an automatic contender for a best-dressed list.

Martina Devlin

The only real firm rule about cross-dressing is that neither sex should ever wear anything they haven't yet figured out how to go to the toilet in.

P.J. O'Rourke

Women are funny. Last Christmas my wife gave me two neckties. I got up on Christmas morning, put one of them on, went downstairs, showed it to her, and the first thing she said was, 'And just what was wrong with the other one?'

Dave Allen

Frank Gormley was what was known as a 'bespoke' tailor. This is an old English word meaning 'ridiculously expensive'.

George Hook

It's easy to spot the best man at a nudist wedding.

Shaun Connors

Why do you keep taking off your clothes? Gay Byrne did *The Late Late* for thirty years and you never even saw his elbows. We see more of your bottom than your face.

Hector Ó hEochagáin's mother to him

In France nobody under eighty wears a beret. Even then I'm sure it's only worn by one of those little old actors employed by the government to walk up and down the streets of deserted towns with a baguette under their arm to give the illusion that there are actually people living there.

Terry Wogan

The garter has hanged more men than the halter.

Dennis O'Keeffe

At an army medical examination the doctor said to me, 'Get your clothes off.' I said, 'Shouldn't you take me out to dinner first?'

Spike Milligan

Asked by a magistrate why he stole 757 sweaters, 733 men's shirts, 460 dresses, 403 jackets, 83 pairs of socks and 286 pairs of children's trousers, worth in all about £14,000, the defendant replied, 'I have a large family.'

Sorcha Kelly

Most women prefer shoes to men because they're reliable, they flatter us, and they're unlikely to run off on another pair of feet.

Anne Marie Scanlon

My child came up to me the other day and said, 'Dad, I'm fifteen now. Can I wear a bra?' I replied, 'Now look here Richard…'

Gene Fitzpatrick

The first naked woman I saw was in the *National Geographic*.

Bob Geldof

She told me that forties fashions were back so I went out and got her a gas-mask.

James McKeon

I used to dress off the peg but then the neighbours started taking their clothes in from the line.

Colin McEvoy

One of the reasons our marriage collapsed was because I could never get his shirts as white as his teeth.

Marguerite McDaid on her ex-husband Jim

Behind every successful businessman stands a wife with nothing to wear.

Hal Roach

The tall blonde told the attendant in the shoe shop that she wanted a pair of flat shoes. 'To wear with what?' he enquired. 'My small, rich boyfriend,' she explained.

Angela O'Connor

A man can wear the same dark suit night after night on live television. He changes the hue of a shirt or pattern of his tie and, behold, sartorial excellence! He pulls a comb through his short-back-and-sides and everyone thinks he's Cary Grant. A woman, on the other hand, is expected to have a vast wardrobe. She has to appear with faultless make-up and a gleaming hairdo or she'll get letters referring to her in terms like 'lazy, greasy-faced cow'.

Deirdre Purcell

My flat in Notting Hill was so cold in winter I had to put on my coat before going to bed. I'd have moved in with any man who had central heating.

Marian Keyes

People who wear cardigans are subversive.

Rita Ann Higgins

He can't think without his hat.

Samuel Beckett

Where do nudists keep their keys to the nudist colony?

Shay Dermody

The only time a man is ever interested in what a woman is wearing is when he's thinking how he might get it off her.

Martina Devlin

My aunts were always knitting me things that never fitted me when I was a child. They always knitted something you'd 'grow into'. Trouble was, by the time I'd grown into it, I'd worn it out.

Dave Allen

To cover up the ticking of our body clocks, we're wearing soundproof knickers on stage tonight.

The Nualas

I was up in Camden market and I saw this guy who wasn't wearing a leather jacket and I thought: 'Poser.'

Sean Hughes

I remember the first time I fell in love. I was fifteen years old and in a department store. Suddenly the breath was knocked from my body as my eyes fixed on the object of my desire – a pair of four-inch, black-patent platform wedges with an ankle strap.

Marian Keyes

Ironing should only be attempted when absolutely necessary; for example when you've run out of money to buy new clothes.

Joe O'Connor

Irish women wouldn't know fashion if it tottered up to them on ten-inch heels.

Paul Costelloe

You have to be tough to work in a frock for forty years.

Danny La Rue

I was once refused entrance to a discotheque because I was wearing trousers. There was only one thing for it. I took them off.

Cliodhna Ní Dhómhnaill

How long have I been wearing a feather boa? Ever since my wife found it in the glove compartment of my car!

Tommy Makem

When English people hear my Irish accent they think I'm the sort of man who would be delivering their laundry.

Brian Moore

The most embarrassing moment of my life was losing my ill-tied shorts in front of hundreds of people while executing a beautiful high dive during an under-15 swimming gala in Spain.

Joe O'Shea

Do you know why they call it a Wonderbra? Because when you take it off, you wonder where your tits went.

Deirdre O'Kane

People who wear creases in their jeans should be phased out. And people who wear loafers without socks. Especially if they have creases in their jeans.

George Carlin

Writing songs is the most fun you can have with your clothes on.

John Waters

She wore a Biblical type dress – low and behold.

Maureen Potter

Two women are talking and one of them says, 'Isn't that Mr Carruthers across the road? Doesn't he dress nicely?' The other says, 'Yes. And very quickly too.'

Dave Allen

For a woman with breasts half way down her body, Susannah should stop slagging off the helpless public and invest in a sturdier bra.

Peaches Geldof on fashion guru Susannah Constantine

What would you do if an epileptic had a fit in your bath? Throw in the washing.

Sean Hughes

You know you've got a problem with shoes if you've just bought them but refuse to wear them because you don't want to damage them.

Marian Keyes

ODIOUS COMPARISONS

Election counts are like being at your own post mortem without an anaesthetic.

Ruairí Quinn

The spa is a religious place full of ceremony and learned behaviour, a bit like Lourdes for lapsed Catholics.

David McWilliams

Einstein's theory of relativity: Time goes a lot slower when you're with relatives.

Joe O'Connor

Geoffrey McGonigle has an arse like two bags of cement.

Joe Brolly

Our health service might have been designed by the people who organised Barbra Streisand's concert at Castletown House.

Con Houlihan

Neil Jordan is the master of the mutter, the Fellini of pained indifference. Getting him to be open is rather like trying to persuade Greta Garbo to go ice-skating in the nude with you in broad daylight.

Barry Egan

The Irish property market is an out-of-control aircraft full of petrified passengers, with neither a pilot nor working controls.

David McWilliams

Ireland called World War Two 'The 'Emergency', making it sound rather like a chip-pan fire.

Paul Howard

My father could shake off the police like the pigeon feathers stuck to his hair.

Frances Cahill on her father Martin, 'The General'

My mother was hostile towards my wife. She thought the sun shone from her boy's *derrière*. If I'd brought home the Virgin Mary, she'd have said her family wasn't good enough.

George Hook

Gay Byrne never forgot he was always on camera so that even if you were boring the arse off the man he would give you that look suggesting you made Einstein seem like a dummy.

Lee Dunne

The first cell phone I owned was about the size of a car battery. It was no good to me because no one I knew had another one.

Conal Gallen

The Virgin Prunes looked like a bunch of pre-Raphaelite serial killers.

Ferdia MacAnna

Trying to bring up children today is a bit like hanging onto an aircraft as it's taking off.

Gabriel Byrne

Just because your wife dies doesn't mean your house won't burn down.

Tom Humphries

The main difference between a man and a boy is the size of the toy.

Ronan Keating

If you don't go to other people's funerals they won't go to yours.

Brian Behan

My idea of exercise is striking a match for a cigarette.

Anne Marie Scanlon

Asking me to advise people about alcohol would be like asking Michael Jackson to talk at a babysitting convention.

David Feherty

In person Enda Kenny is impressive, even charismatic, but on radio and TV he comes across as an overcooked ham.

John Waters

I always loved the ugly red-brick streets of Belfast more than Manchester or Los Angeles.

George Best

Thunder is God trying to parallel park.

Graham Norton

May I suggest a ban on World Cup blather on *Questions & Answers*: it's as yucky as your grandmother slipping her tongue in when she kisses you goodnight.

Tom Humphries

Playing for Sunderland is a bit like playing for Ireland. We drink a lot and run around like nutters.

Jason McAteer

A Shi'ite effort.

David Feherty on a poor shot he played in the Dubai Classic

There are rumours of motorists going missing for days on the infamous Red Cow roundabout, the Bermuda triangle of the M50.

David McWilliams

Garret FitzGerald ran his government like a university debating society.

Frank Dunlop

There's a better chance of getting the wrinkles out of a bloodhound's face than out of 100% linen shirts.

Marian Keyes

If Daniel O'Donnell were a drug addict, a drunkard and a sex maniac he'd be the darling of the media.

Fr Brian D'Arcy

Ronnie Drew's voice always sounded like he was gargling with gravel.

Gerry Ryan

My aunt always said divorce was worse than murder.

Edna O'Brien

For Wimbledon to compete in the Premiership with our finances is like going into a nuclear war with bows and arrows.

Joe Kinnear

RTE is the only state company that carries more passengers than CIE.

John Boland

The German language sounds like typewriters eating tinfoil.

Dylan Moran

She was about as moving as Imelda Marcos pleading for a new pair of shoes.

Michael Redmond on Madonna's efforts to portray a missionary in _Shanghai Surprise_

I want you to hoof the ball out of defence rather than fannying about the way you do with Arsenal.

Jack Charlton to Dave O'Leary

The Fo£ding $tuff

The insurance man called this morning. He said if the last instalment on granny's funeral isn't paid, up she comes.

Frank Carson

When I'm 65 I know I'll be entitled to a free television licence. I haven't got a TV so could I arrange to get the cash instead, or else could I have vouchers for smoked salmon?

Pat Ingoldsby

What will I do with the money? I think I'll go out and buy a new kitchen.

Anne Enright after winning the Booker Prize in 2007

Once during a conversation in a pub, no one could get the answer to a particular question so George hailed a taxi and returned to his flat in Chelsea to check it in a book. He then made the journey back to the pub. I think the fare was £100.

Barbara Best on her famous brother

I've been travelling a lot recently and it's starting to catch up with me. My mother gave me a lift home the other day and as I got out of the car I threw ten euro at her and said 'Keep the change.'

Olaf Tyaransen

You're a millionaire if you have your health.

Dickie Rock

Never lend anyone money for plastic surgery. You won't be able to recognise them when it comes time to collect.

Shaun Connors

In recent years the financial body clock has taken over from the traditional one of having babies.

David McWilliams

I have to laugh when I see stars like Colin Farrell driving around town in an old banger, wearing torn jeans. If an ordinary guy did that he'd he called a bloody skanger but Farrell can get away with it because people know he has a few bob.

Dickie Rock

How do you make a small fortune on Broadway? Start off with a big one.

Marion McKeone

Anyone that ever got money out of a priest ought to have a statue put up to them.

Frank O'Connor

I recently bought a book of free verse for twelve dollars.

George Carlin

They spent £6 million on The Spike. What's the point?

Mary Mannion

They've done so many spreads on me in the *Sunday World*, some people think I have shares in the place.

Yvonne Costelloe

Retirement means twice the husband on half the money.

Sean McCarthy

My parents were poor but honest – which is why they were poor.

Bill Kelly

Men want an ideal beauty. Women want big spenders.

Martina Devlin

In spite of the cost of living it's still very popular.

Noel Purcell

I heard a charity appeal on the radio the other day that said it only takes ten euros a week to support a child in Africa. I'm thinking of moving my whole family out there.

Patrick Donovan

The main difference between sex for money and sex for free is that sex for money usually costs a lot less.

Brendan Francis

The real bank robbers are those who work in them.

Dermot Morgan

My earliest ambition was to be a bus conductor. It wasn't the glamour that appealed to me but the money. I thought they got to keep it all.

Tom Doorley

If you go into a campus these days, people are too busy reading *The Wall Street Journal* to protest.

Fionnuala Flanagan

The judge said to the plaintiff at a divorce hearing, 'I'm awarding your wife 100 euro a week.' 'Thanks, Your Honour,' he replied, 'I'll try and throw in a few bob myself.'

Shaun Connors

Basically all we want to do is earn as much money as possible for doing fuck all.

Shane MacGowan in 1977

Politicians take their money into the bank through the back door. I take it out through the roof.

Martin Cahill

The next time Bertie Ahern wants a few bob he should avoid being a Manchester martyr. A better option would be to put out the Bertie Bowl at Lansdowne.

David Shanley

My first priority is to fix the car.

John Connolly after receiving a £350,000 advance for his first book

It's difficult to motivate players who earn 40 grand a week, have three Mercs, and mistresses everywhere.

Joe Kinnear

For most of my time in RTE I was terrified to ask for a pay rise in case they fired me.

Gay Byrne

In normal life you get gifts from your friends and take loans from strangers. Bertie Ahern got loans from his friends and gifts from strangers.

Pat Rabbitte on Bertiegate

Writing is the only talent I have that doesn't involve working for tips.

Kate Holmquist

Women never threw knickers at our gigs. We'd have preferred if they threw pound notes.

Paddy Cole

Long ago I discovered that teaching is an easy way of earning a living provided that one doesn't make the mistake of actually teaching.

George Ryan

First Communion and Confirmation in Ireland produce a stupendous outpouring of beneficence which is spelled C-A-S-H.

David Monaghan

Not only do I love her, I worship the ground her father struck oil on.

Frank Carson

Being a doctor is a great job. He tells a woman to take off all her clothes. Then he examines her and sends her husband a bill for €50.

Shaun Connors

If you pee standing up, you're worth an extra fifth in the salary department.

Eddie Hobbs

This whole world is all wrong if you're unfortunate enough to be a poor auld fella. Which at least half of you will be one of these days, whether you like it or not.

Declan Lynch

Look at Hollywood: How many stories have we heard of women who put their ambitions on hold in order to support their actor husband through the lean years, only to be abandoned as soon as the money begins to roll in? 'Thanks a million for working three crappy jobs while I went to auditions. I'm off now with that anorexic one with the fake knockers and bee-stung lips over there, but hey, I'll always speak fondly of you in *People* interviews.'

Marian Keyes

You can live 'with' people who are poor, but you can't live 'like' them. If I get depressed in Ballymun my provincial has me over in Milltown the next day. If I get sick he has me in the Mater Private. Whereas if somebody in Ballymun gets sick they may have to wait a year for that operation.

Peter McVerry

Miscellaneous

Psychoanalysis is the most stupendous confidence trick of the century.

Anthony Clare

There are some people who want to throw their arms around you simply because it's Christmas, and other people who want to strangle you because it's Christmas.

Robert Lynd

The secret of success is to fail better.

Samuel Beckett

A learned old schoolmaster in Cork was once described to me as a man who could spit in nine languages.

Maurice Healy

Don't read your publicity. Weigh it.

Albert Reynolds

Confusion is not an ignoble condition.

Brian Friel

Experts, by definition, are conspirators against common sense.

John Waters

The price of Prozac went up 50% last year. When users were asked how they felt about the hike they said, 'Whatever...'

Conan O'Brien

After every horror we're told, 'Now the healing can begin.' No. There's just a pause before the next horror.

George Carlin

The two oldest professions in the world are spoiled by amateurs.

Paddy Mallon

The enemy of appreciating art of any kind is to feel you must say something clever about it.

Vincent Dowling

Never run anything or anyone down to a person you don't know. Statistics show that nine times out of ten the person you're speaking to will be the mother/sister/best friend of the one you're bitching about. This is very bad for your health, especially if they deck you.

Anne Marie Scanlon

I always sit in the back seats of planes. I never heard of one reversing into a mountain.

Conal Gallen

'Legend' is a euphemism for 'Past it', 'Over the hill' and 'Forgotten but not gone'.

Terry Wogan

Crying isn't proof of a great capacity to feel. It's proof of a great capacity to cry.

Dylan Moran

Even the humblest man has dignity at his funeral.

Con Houlihan

My cross in life is arthritis but I don't talk about it. Most people are bored by your problems. My father always told me that the phrase 'How are you?' is a greeting, not a question.

Maeve Binchy

One consolation about memory loss in old age is that you also forget a lot of things you didn't intend to remember in the first place.

George Carlin

There's only one problem about instant gratification: it takes too long.

Owen O'Neill

Surgeons' mistakes get buried, architects' ones get built.

Ruairí Quinn

Critics are clampers who can't drive.

John Waters

I was in Dublin recently for my father's 103rd birthday party. He wasn't there himself. He died when he was 36.

Dusty Young

My mother is determined to master the new technology. She typed an email to me on the computer, printed it out, popped it in an envelope and posted it to me.

John O'Farrell

I went to the doctor and he told me I was suffering from hypochondria. 'Not that as well!' I said.

Jimmy O'Dea

Sibling squabbles are more vicious than disputes between strangers.

Sam Smyth

Did you hear about the man who reversed into a car boot sale and sold his engine?

Frank Carson

It's a strange thing about the Moriartys. They never mind too much about dying, but they hate growing old.

Joe O'Toole

It's official: Nicorette is the best cure for nicotine addiction. Just put a patch over each eye and you won't be able to find your cigarettes.

Brendan O'Carroll

If fifty is the new forty, does that mean that when you're 12 you're still looking for your soother?

Stephen Byrne

We are what we are, but we're also what we were.

Sean Boylan

Yesterday is a memory, tomorrow is a mystery. Today is a gift, and that's why they call it the present.

Daniel O'Donnell

The Evening Herald says a man is knocked down by a car every three hours. He must be getting fed up of it.

Shaun Connors

A breakdown can lead to a breakthrough.

Stephen Costello

My wife says I live in the past and I say, 'When I look at the present, the past's not too bad.'

Jim Patton

Is there one of us who is not confused?

Paul Durcan

It's partly knowing that it's not going to last that makes happiness so wonderful.

Shane MacGowan

The main problem with housework is that six months later you have to do it all over again.

Rosaleen Linehan

I really don't have any interest in the middle class.

Peter McVerry

The most embarrassing moment of my life was when a caller told me on live radio that I had a voice like honey dripping on nipples.

Brenda Power

When you're in the last ditch, the only thing left is to sing.

Samuel Beckett

Life is a mess. We don't remember being born, and death isn't an experience, so all we have is this chaotic middle bit bristling with loose ends in which nothing is ever properly finished or done with.

John Banville

Publicity can't be switched off. There's always someone hiding in the bushes.

Ronan Keating

'If you don't go to school and learn your lessons,' Brian Moore's mother told him, 'you'll be good for nothing but opening car doors and holding umbrellas over old ladies.'

Patricia Craig

The family is a war zone. And that's when it's functioning reasonably well!

Patricia Redlich

People who tell me I can't do something only make me work twice as hard. I use negativity as rocket fuel.

Michael Flatley

How do I sum up my life as an analyst? I can only quote the words of David Brent, star of *The Office*: 'Accept that some days you are the pigeon, and some days you are the statue.'

Pat Spillane

Be nice to people on the way up because you'll meet them again on the way down. Only when that time comes you'll be travelling twice as fast.

Jimmy Higgins

I could always guarantee that the Irish Citizen Army would fight to the death. But I couldn't guarantee they'd be on time.

James Connolly

A bypass saved my life. I don't want to have a heart attack – only an art attack.

Mike Murphy

There's a thin line between loyalty and stupidity.

Roy Keane

I reckon we're all made up of equal parts Rambo and Lucille Ball.

Boy George

I'm not that worried about growing old. Largely because it beats the alternative.

Paddy Murray

If you think nobody cares if you're alive or not, try missing a few mortgage payments.

Pat Flanagan

Every day is a lost opportunity.

Stephen Rea

Find a job you enjoy and you'll never have to work again.

Bernie Comaskey

The people who are the best at what they do are also the nicest. It's the ones who are only half way up the ladder that have the egos.

Ronan Keating

We should never say to latecomers that they're in perfect time when the meal is stuck to the roof of the oven and the other guests are legless with pre-dinner drinks.

Maeve Binchy

I'm thinking of setting up an Association for Non-Members. It'll have no rules and won't meet once a month. People will ring us and ask us for our reaction to the news of the day and we'll say, 'No comment, but don't quote us on that.'

Kevin Marron

The only time I feel fully relaxed at a party is when I'm in the bathroom.

Pat Ingoldsby

No human being ever believes any other human being has a right to be in bed when he himself is up.

Robert Lynd

We are born at the rise of the curtain and we die with its fall, and every night in the presence of our patrons we write our new creation, and every night it is blotted out forever. So what use is it to say to audience or critic: 'Ah, but you should have seen me last Tuesday.'

Mícheál Mac Liammóir

To be relevant is a lot harder than to be successful.

Bono

It might or might not be right to kill, but sometimes it's necessary.

Gerry Adams

The typical west of Ireland family consists of father, mother, twelve children and resident Dutch anthropologist.

Flann O'Brien

There are two different realities in our society: You get people using cocaine on Saturday night and eating organic food on Sunday.

Archbishop Diarmuid Martin

My father wasn't very well educated. The first time he saw Brussels sprouts he said, 'Who made a balls of the cabbage?'

Big O

You don't have to be idiotically happy all the time. I mean, if you were, there'd be nothing to look forward to, would there?

Ardal O'Hanlon

Life sucks and then you croak.

Jason Byrne

Index